MARRIAGE

The Mystery of Christ and the Church

Third edition

David J. Engelsma

REFORMED
FREE PUBLISHING
ASSOCIATION
Jenison, Michigan

First edition 1975: *Marriage: The Mystery of Christ and the Church*

Revised edition 1998: *Marriage, the Mystery of Christ and the Church: The Covenant-Bond in Scripture and History*

Third edition 2014: *Marriage: The Mystery of Christ and the Church*

Scripture quotations are taken from the Authorized (King James) Version

Cover design by Erika Kiel
Interior design by Katherine Lloyd, The DESK

Reformed Free Publishing Association
1894 Georgetown Center Drive
Jenison, MI 49428
www.rfpa.org
mail@rfpa.org

ISBN 978-1-936054-51-0
Ebook ISBN 978-1-936054-46-6
LCCN 2014955953

To my father and mother
and to Ruth

"This is one of those books that you wish could be put into the hands of every married couple and those contemplating marriage…If the contents of this book were put into practice, society would become more stable and broken homes would be few and far between."

—*The Gospel Witness*

"…one of the finest among the flood of such books flowing off the presses…The book [has] a theological depth and seriousness often lacking in non-Reformed books on this subject."

—*Reformed Herald*

"A book that says many biblical things about sex, children, family, the mystery of marriage. Recommended for laypersons and preachers alike."

—*The Reformed Journal*

"This book does faithfully reflect the teachings of God's Word on marriage."

—*The Banner*

"A pastor, husband, and father speaks of marriage and its relationships in terms that few want to hear today–even in the church."

—*Moody*

"…there is much to be learned from this book for it touches upon much where the rubber hits the road in marriage. The chapters 'The Christian Man as Husband' and 'The Christian Woman as

Wife' serve as excellent mirrors and may also serve the reader to discover where he or she fails in honouring the special God-designed role in marriage."

—*Trowel and Sword*

"If ever there is a book which is vital reading for the church in our day, it is this one...This book is essential reading...and particularly should it be part of the staple diet offered to young people contemplating marriage...[This book] challenged my views on the vexed subject of divorce and remarriage...[it] also caused me to re-examine my whole attitude to marriage in general and my own marriage in particular, and to re-appraise my role as husband, lover and head of the family."

—*British Reformed Journal*

"...Engelsma's book is ideal for any who has an interest in the subject...Ministers, elders, deacons, husbands, wives, parents, young people, and engaged couples, especially engaged couples, should read it. They will do so with life-long profit."

—*The Tamar Reformed Witness*

"...Engelsma...presents a rich, biblically based view of marriage."

—*New Oxford Review*

"...Engelsma...provides what may well be the clearest expression of God's heart on the matter of marriage in print today. In simple, readable form, the author sets out the biblical view of marriage."

—Charles Crisimier III in the *Standard Bearer*

Contents

• Section One •

THE BIBLICAL GOSPEL OF MARRIAGE

• Section Two •

A BRIEF HISTORY OF THE
CHURCH'S DOCTRINE OF MARRIAGE

Preface to the Third Edition

*M*arriage, *the Mystery of Christ and the Church* was born not in the cool atmosphere of theological academia, but in the heat of the pastoral ministry.

Having just graduated from seminary and having just entered upon the pastoral ministry in my first congregation, with no special interest in marriage other than that I had recently married, I found myself, willy-nilly, in a cauldron of congregational discord regarding remarriage after divorce.

The very existence of the congregation seemed to be in jeopardy. To reject the remarriage by Christian discipline threatened the continuing existence of the congregation. To accept the remarriage bid fair to bring down on the church the wrath of God.

Some fifty years later, I keenly remember concluding, not without fear and trepidation, before the face of God in my study, "If we go down, we will go down with the word of God."

The result was the series of sermons on marriage, divorce, and remarriage that basically became the content of the first part of this book.

The church did not "go down." She endured the attack on her by Satan, which was also God's trial of her faith. She emerged with clear, strong conviction concerning the truth of marriage, as did also her pastor.

That was some fifty years ago.

The passing of the years, and in them many struggles as a

minister with difficult marital circumstances attendant on a pastoral ministry, have not weakened my conviction in the slightest concerning the biblical truth of marriage that this book proclaims and defends.

Indeed, my conviction has become stronger.

Marriage, as an unutterably precious and potent ordinance of God, is lifelong. The reality that marriage was designed by the Creator to symbolize, namely, the covenant of God in Jesus Christ with the elect church, demands it. The Bible passages teach it. The stand of the early church confirms it. The Christian family pleads for it. The onlooking, adulterous world requires it, if only as a witness against the world, so that God may be just when he judges.

Strange as the word of this book must seem, not only to the ungodly, but also to the majority of evangelicals, Presbyterians, and Reformed today—a word of sexual purity, marital fidelity, and the keeping of one's marriage vows to his or her own hurt and loss—it is a word that they almost desperately need to hear. This is the word of God on marriage, divorce, and remarriage, cutting through the babble—the *religious* babble—that is nothing more than the prostituting of holy marriage to the whims, wishes, and will of fornicating, adulterous men and women.

The book is strong medicine. Such medicine is required by the grievous marital sickness of our time. The church that fails to administer this medicine in our day is no servant of the great physician.

The second part of the book, although an integral part of the book's advocacy of marriage as the mystery of Christ and the church, consists of a brief overview of the New Testament church's doctrine of marriage, from soon after the apostles to the present day. Not without pain to the author, this part of the book necessarily includes sharp criticism of the Reformed tradition, going back to John Calvin.

But the history of marriage doctrine and practice that constitutes the second part of the book also demonstrates that the truth of marriage proclaimed in the first part of the book is by no means lacking in strong support in the history of the church.

—DAVID J. ENGELSMA
Hudsonville, Michigan
November 2014

Preface to the Revised Edition

The main change in this revised edition—and a significant and lengthy change it is—is the addition of a new section consisting of a history of the church's doctrine of marriage.

This is section two of the new edition and accounts for the added subtitle: *The Covenant-Bond in Scripture and History.* The history will serve several purposes in connection with the gospel, or doctrine, of marriage that is the content of section one. First, it will demonstrate that the doctrine of marriage, divorce, and remarriage set forth in section one is not novel. It is, essentially, the doctrine that the early church taught for some one thousand years after the apostles.

Second, it will both acknowledge (regretfully) that the doctrine of marriage set forth in these pages differs from the teaching of the reformers and point out (again regretfully) the error of the reformers' teaching.

Third, it will confront Protestants, especially those who are evangelical, Reformed, or Presbyterian, with the certain, appalling consequences of a doctrine of marriage that rejects the truth of a lifelong, indissoluble bond. This is the burden of the chapter "Contemporary Lawlessness." No Christian can be at peace with what he or she sees taking place in the churches and in his or her own family at the end of the twentieth century. It is a scandal. Divorce with the remarriage that inevitably follows is hurtful to the people, especially the children. It is offensive to those outside the churches. It dishonors the triune God and Father of Jesus Christ. What is worse is that the churches and their theologians are approving the scandal in the name of the triune God and Father of Jesus Christ.

Revision made possible minor, mostly grammatical and stylistic corrections and improvements in the original work: what now becomes section one. The content remains the same. For the most part, even those references that date the first printing of the book (1975) are retained. They do not detract from the instruction. At the very least, they show that a Reformed preacher has his eye on current events, as well as on the timeless, and always timely, word of God.

There is one exception. In the past twenty-odd years, I have come to see clearly that the reason for the wife's departing in 1 Corinthians 7:10–11 is the fornication of her husband. This bears heavily, of course, on the question whether the innocent party may remarry. Indeed, this understanding of the passage is decisive for the question. The observant reader will notice that this development is reflected in chapter 8.

The publisher thought it fitting that a new, revised edition come into the world in appropriate dress. Hence the fresh book design. New subheadings within chapters were supplied by the author.

My desire is that the Spirit of Christ will use the book to strengthen married saints, to instruct the younger generation, and to fight, indeed destroy, without compromise, the other mind on marriage in the churches.

—DAVID J. ENGELSMA
Grandville, Michigan
September 1998

Preface to the First Edition

Before this book was published, it was preached. The contents of the book are, substantially, a series of sermons that were preached on marriage during my pastorate in Loveland, Colorado.

I am convinced that the one great need of God's people regarding marriage is a better knowledge of the word of God. Consequently, this book was born out of the needs of the congregation and out of the wrestlings of the pastorate. The sermons were preached with the practical purpose that the married and youth alike might know and honor God's institution of marriage. The book is published with the same desire. May God use it to glorify himself through a people faithful in marriage.

I express thanks to my wife, who encouraged me to prepare the material for publication and who did the typing—proving herself in this, too, a *help*.

—DAVID J. ENGELSMA
South Holland, Illinois
July 1974

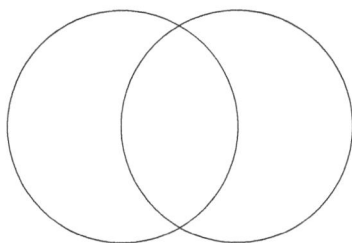

Section One

THE BIBLICAL GOSPEL OF MARRIAGE

1

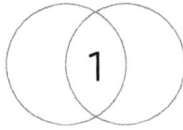

The Mystery of Marriage

For this cause shall a man leave his father and mother, and shall he joined unto his wife, and they two shall be one flesh. This is a great mystery: but I speak concerning Christ and the church. —Ephesians 5:31–32

The rampant godlessness of our society is indicated by the frequency and ease of divorce and remarriage. Our society makes a mockery of marriage and its vows of fidelity. The state is in the process of removing all legal restraints. We have come to take divorce for granted. It is almost as common as the marriage that preceded it. Nevertheless, the corruption of marriage takes its toll. A price is paid. This corrupting of marriage is the cause of fearful evils that even society cannot ignore or minimize. There is the bitter misery of soul that shatters those who have been unfaithful and that leads to drink, drugs, nervous breakdowns, and even suicide. There is the presence of a lawless breed of young people (with no race excluded), which seriously threatens the very existence of the state itself. The foundation of the state is the home, and the cornerstone of the home is the marriage relation of a man and his wife.

The evils that corrupt marriage also tend to infect the church. We are susceptible to the mentality and practices of the world. The thermometer of the growing coldness of the church can well be the extent to which she permits marriage to be defiled in her fellowship. For this reason it is necessary that the truth of marriage be preached in the congregation.

Even apart from the strong threat from the world, there are always hardships that trouble married people in the church. Some do not like the Reformed marriage form because it begins on such a gloomy note:

> Whereas married persons are generally, by reason of sin, subject to many troubles and afflictions; to the end that you N. and N....may also be assured in your hearts of the certain assistance of God in your afflictions, hear therefore from the Word of God, how honorable the marriage state is, and that it is an institution of God, which is pleasing to Him.[1]

However, for this very reason it is a good form. It is realistic, at a time when we are prone to be looking at marriage through rose-tinted glasses. There are "many troubles and afflictions" in marriage—the marriage of believers included. This is another reason we need to hear God's word concerning marriage.

In addition marriage has been given an important place and function within the church by God. It has a positive, practical significance for the welfare of the congregation of Christ.

---

1 Form for the Confirmation of Marriage before the Church, in *The Confessions and the Church Order of the Protestant Reformed Churches* (Grandville, MI: Protestant Reformed Churches in America, 2005), 306.

Godly marriage and the godly home are the church's strongholds. To maintain these strongholds we must hear and obey God's word on marriage.

In light of these considerations, it is urgent that faithful preachers of the gospel bring God's word on marriage to God's people. It must be God's word that is proclaimed. We may not bring man's wisdom on marital matters to the church. We may not share with her the fine insights into marriage that we have obtained through our extensive experience. For regarding marriage also, the wisdom of men is foolishness with God. But by the grace of the Holy Spirit we must speak the word of God on marriage, as God has revealed it in the scriptures.

The Intimacy of Marriage

God calls marriage the mystery of Christ and the church: "This is a great mystery: but I speak concerning Christ and the church" (Eph. 5:32).

In Ephesians 5:22–31 the apostle has been giving instruction about the mutual behavior of husbands and wives, taking as the pattern, or standard, the conduct of Christ with regard to the church and the conduct of the church with regard to Christ. One cannot help but notice that this beautiful description of marriage immediately follows the description of the dark and sordid wickedness of verses 3–12: fornication, uncleanness, filthiness, foolish talking, and things done in secret that are a shame even to mention. There the ugly perversion of marriage was exposed and condemned. Here, in contrast, the beautiful truth is displayed and exhorted. Paul has been telling wives and husbands how to live with each other in marriage. Wives are called to submit; husbands are called to love. The standard that he gives for this behavior is the relationship between Christ and the church. Wives must submit "as the church is subject unto Christ" (v. 24). Husbands must love their wives "even as Christ also loved the church" (v. 25).

Then Paul begins to teach the closeness of man and woman in marriage, again as patterned by the closeness of Christ and the church. This closeness is mentioned in verse 28: "So ought men to love their wives as their own bodies. He that loveth his wife loveth himself." A man's wife is part of himself. Therefore, for a man to hate his own wife is as strange as it is for him to hate his own flesh (v. 29). For this is what his wife is: she is part of his flesh. Immediately the apostle declares that this is the case according to the standard of Christ and the church. After he has written, "For no man ever yet hated his own flesh; but nourisheth and cherisheth it," he adds, "even as the Lord the church" (v. 29). The reason the Lord does not hate, but nourishes and cherishes the church is given in verse 30: "For we are members of his body, of his flesh, and of his bones." This is to say, we are part of him.

Right at this point Paul quotes from Genesis. Verse 31 of Ephesians 5 is a quotation, almost verbatim, of Genesis 2:24, which reads: "Therefore shall a man leave his father and his mother, and shall cleave unto his wife: and they shall be one flesh." This text is the word spoken by God after he had created Eve and presented her to Adam and after Adam had named her. When Adam received his wife from God, he said, "This is now bone of my bones, and flesh of my flesh: she shall be called Woman, because she was taken out of Man" (Gen. 2:23). Then follow the words quoted by Paul in Ephesians 5:31. These are not words that Adam spoke at that occasion, but they are words that God inspired Moses to write down later as his own divine commentary on what had occurred, namely, the institution of marriage. That this is the proper view of Genesis 2:24 is proved by Jesus' statement in Matthew 19:4–5 that the one who made man and woman in the beginning said, "For this cause shall a man leave father and mother."

God's commentary on marriage teaches the amazing intimacy of the marriage bond. It is fitting that Paul should quote the text that teaches this intimacy of the marriage relationship at that point where he has asserted that a woman is part of a man, just as we are members of Christ's body.

The intimacy of marriage is shown, first, by the fact that the marriage bond takes precedence over the relationship between parent and child. A man leaves his father and mother for his wife. The relation of parents and child is the closest natural blood tie. More is meant by leaving father and mother than merely getting out of their house. The bond of marriage supersedes the parent-child relationship. It should do this. A man must leave father and mother when he marries, and the same holds for a young woman. If a person fails to leave his parents, perhaps with the connivance of the parents, there will be trouble in the marriage. He is, as the saying goes, still "tied to mother's apron strings." Implied in this is the superiority of marriage over the parent-child relationship, particularly in its closeness, its intimacy. This is amazing. For the parent-child relation is strong and close. The child is the blood and flesh of the parents, whereas there is no blood tie between the man and his wife.

The second way God stresses the closeness of the bond of marriage is his use of the word translated as "joined" in Genesis 2:24 and Ephesians 5:31. Literally the word means "to be glued to someone, to stick closely to someone." It is expressive of the closest possible relationship. A man is glued to his wife so that he sticks to her.

It is especially the declaration "and they shall be one flesh" (Gen. 2:24) that shows the amazing intimacy of marriage. Here is the astounding thing. Paul recognized this as he looked at Genesis 2:24. He wanted to make sure that we see this also. Therefore, under the guidance of the Spirit, he made a change in the text as he quoted it. In Genesis the word *two* does not appear; we read only, "And they shall be one flesh." What is implicit in the text in Genesis, Paul makes explicit by inserting the word "two": "And they two shall be one flesh." Thus he emphasizes that the intimacy of marriage is such that two become one. It is not even the closeness of two glued closely together, for even in this case there are still two. In marriage there are no longer two, but one. This was Jesus' analysis in Matthew 19:6: "Wherefore they are no more twain, but one flesh."

It is misunderstanding of the phrase "they two shall be one flesh" to limit it to the bodily oneness of the sexual relationship. This interpretation is mistaken on two counts. First, "one flesh" refers to more than oneness of body. Second, the sexual relationship in marriage not only involves oneness of body but also oneness of soul. "One flesh" refers to the becoming one of the entire nature of the man and the woman. There is oneness of bodies and souls, of thinking and desiring, of hopes and disappointments, of labors and goals. There is oneness of the whole of earthly life; the husband and wife share one life.

When we have said all this, we have still not explained the intimacy of marriage exhaustively. In the end, the reality of the oneness of marriage is incomprehensible. Marriage is mysterious. Just as we do not comprehend the conception of a child, or life itself, so we do not comprehend that two are "no more twain, but one flesh." The inspired writer therefore says in amazement, "There be three things which are too wonderful for me, yea, four which I know not...and the way of a man with a maid" (Prov. 30:18–19). The reason for the mysterious depths of marriage is that in marriage God is at work. It is not the case that in marriage a man joins himself to his wife. Rather, he is joined to his wife by another. That other is God. The glue of marriage is God's glue, as the act of applying it is God's act. This is why, as we will see, only God can, and only God may, dissolve the marriage bond. Consequently, a marriage ceremony is a solemn occasion. The solemnity is this: God is making two into one flesh. The deliberate attack upon the solemnity of marriage on the part of some young people today, by marrying barefooted, in slovenly attire, and to the strains of frivolous folk tunes, is part of the general war against marriage as an institution of God.

There are at hand evidences of the amazing intimacy of marriage. One such evidence is the misery of those who separate themselves from their mates, probably in order to unite themselves with others. Even the world notices their "guilt feelings" and their "mental distress." Another indication of the intimacy of marriage is the unique, incommunicable sorrow and pain of the widower or the widow at the death of wife or husband. They simply cannot describe their grief. How does one describe what it is to die in part, but still to go on living?

Marriage as Symbol

In reference now to marriage, particularly from the viewpoint of the amazing intimacy of marriage, Paul says, "This is a great mystery" (Eph. 5:32). He calls marriage a mystery; he calls it a great mystery. We usually designate a *mystery* as something we cannot figure out. Accordingly, we would understand this statement of the apostle to mean that the marriage of a man and a woman has depths that we cannot plumb. However, in scripture the word *mystery* has a distinct meaning. Mystery is God's eternal plan of salvation that is hidden and secret and that man cannot find out or even imagine. But God has now revealed it in Jesus Christ by the gospel so that we who believe can and do know the mystery. The usage of scripture makes this meaning of mystery clear: "It is given unto you to know the mysteries of the kingdom of heaven" (Matt. 13:11). Ephesians 1:9 reads, "Having made known unto us the mystery of his will." A great mystery, therefore, is not a very deep problem, something that is exceedingly puzzling, but it is the salvation of God, which is very marvelous and wonderful.

"But," someone will object, "the marriage of a man and a woman is not the great salvation of God. And this is what Paul is talking about, for he says, 'This is a great mystery'" (Eph. 5:32). Our reply is that Paul is not talking about the marriage of a man and a woman, for he goes on to say, "but I speak concerning Christ and the church." Nevertheless, as he speaks concerning Christ and the church, he still has human marriage in mind. For human marriage is a sign, a divinely ordained symbol, of the relationship of Christ and the church. The underlying reality of marriage is the union of Christ and the church. The fundamental significance of marriage is that it pictures the marriage of Christ and his bride, the church.

Between the Son of God in our flesh, Jesus, and the church, there is the most intimate relationship—so intimate in nature that the two become one. This is the amazing salvation that God planned from eternity and makes known in the gospel. This union of Christ and the church is spoken of in the preceding verses in Ephesians 5. Verse 23 calls Christ the church's head, and it calls the church his body. Verse 30 says that we are members of his body, of his flesh, and of his bones. This is also taught elsewhere in the New Testament. In John 17 Christ prays for the unity of the church, which is, first, our oneness with Christ: "I in them" (v. 23). Paul declares in Galatians 2:20 that "Christ liveth in me." Ephesians 3:17 points out that the realization of salvation is "that Christ may dwell in your hearts by faith." In this way we are "filled with all the fulness of God" (v. 19). Colossians 1:26–27 is very plain when it says that the mystery hid from ages, but now made manifest to the saints, is "Christ in you." The union of Christ and the church takes place when we are regenerated by the Spirit. The sign of this union is baptism, for we are baptized into Christ. We experience this union in faith.

There was a foreshadowing of this great mystery in the Old Testament, which presents the relationship between Jehovah and Israel as a marriage. Jehovah was Israel's husband, and Israel was his wife. Her spiritual faithlessness was adultery (Ezek. 16). Her future perfection is described as betrothal to Jehovah and marriage (Hosea 2). The Song of Solomon vividly sets forth the relationship between Christ and the church in terms of the ecstatic love of marriage. Psalm 45 prophesies the marriage of Christ the king, who is God himself, to a Gentile woman. The Old Testament foretells the mystery of the union of Christ and the church and describes that union as a marriage.

Marriage is a fitting symbol of the relationship between Christ and the church. The woman was not made first, but second. She was made for Adam, and not Adam for her. So also in the counsel of God, not the church, but Christ is first. Christ does not exist for the church, but the church exists for the sake of Christ, to serve and to praise him forever. In the beginning the woman had her origin from the man. Similarly, the church has her origin from Christ. By his atoning blood and by his Spirit and Word, he has created her. Because of the woman's creation from the man and for the man, she can sustain the intimate relation to him that she has as wife. Genesis 2:24, which speaks of the amazing intimacy of marriage, begins with the word "therefore." It bases the intimacy of marriage on the preparation of the woman, as that preparation is recorded in verses 21–23. The same thing is true of the church. The church can be Christ's bride because God has fitted her for Christ in his eternal counsel and because God has formed her by Christ's own Spirit. Finally, marriage is an intimate union. In marriage man is male and female (Gen. 1:27); the two are one. In the mystery of salvation, Christ is the head, and the church is the body. The two are one.

A High Doctrine of Marriage

Since we see marriage as the mystery of Christ and the church, we have a high estimation of marriage: not of my marriage or your marriage or even believers' marriages, but of the institution of marriage. Any estimation of marriage that lacks this regard for it as the God-ordained symbol of Christ and the church is too low. Some in the world may still claim to honor marriage, but lacking this regard they dishonor it. Inevitably, every kind of corruption must ensue.

We are called to regulate our marriages according to the standard of Christ and the church. This is Paul's teaching in Ephesians 5.

It is this that will make for true happiness in marriage. But happiness is not the main thing. In fact, adherence to God's standard for marriage will mean severe affliction for some. Some are eunuchs for the kingdom's sake (Matt. 19:12). The main thing is that we remain faithful to God and to his law governing the institution of marriage.

As a result of our high estimation of marriage, we are convicted daily of our great sinfulness in the matter of our marriages. We are unable to flatter ourselves because we treat our wives or husbands as well as, or better than, most people treat their mates.

The question by which we are judged is, "Did you today behave toward your wife as Christ behaves toward his church?" Or as wives, the question must be faced, "Did you live with your husband as the church is called to live with Christ?" Thus our high estimation of marriage has the effect that we confess our sins and shortcomings in marriage and that we repent.

At the same time the marriage of Christ and the church provides us with a goal toward which we press in our marriages. We strive to pattern our marriages after it. We struggle to reflect in our earthly marriages the heavenly one between Christ, the bridegroom, and the church, his bride. This is the glory and beauty of marriage.

Only believing children of God can accomplish this. Only they know and care about marriage as the symbol of the union of Christ and the church. Only they have Christ dwelling within them so that they are able to fulfill their calling in marriage, whether by loving their wives or by submitting to their husbands. Only they respond, willingly and joyfully, to the word of Jesus Christ: magnify me and the great mystery of my marriage with my people in your marriages.

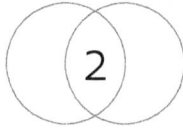

2

The Institution of Marriage

And the LORD God said, It is not good that the man should be alone; I will make him an help meet for him. And out of the ground the LORD God formed every beast of the field, and every fowl of the air; and brought them unto Adam to see what he would call them: and whatsoever Adam called every living creature, that was the name thereof. And Adam gave names to all cattle, and to the fowl of the air, and to every beast of the field; but for Adam there was not found an help meet for him. And the LORD God caused a deep sleep to fall upon Adam, and he slept: and he took one of his ribs, and closed up the flesh instead thereof; And the rib, which the LORD God had taken from man, made he a woman, and brought her unto the man. And Adam said, This is now bone of my bones, and flesh of my flesh: she shall be called Woman, because she was taken out of Man. Therefore shall a man leave his father and his mother, and shall cleave unto his wife: and they shall be one flesh. And they were both naked, the man and his wife, and were not ashamed. —Genesis 2:18–25

At that point in the creation of the world referred to by this text, there was one thing wrong with the creation: there was no woman in it. It was the sixth day of the creation week. Already on this day God had created the animals. He had made the man, Adam, from the dust of the ground. He had set him in the garden of Eden and had given him the command to cultivate the garden and the prohibition against eating of the tree of the knowledge of good and evil. Then God declared that one creature was lacking to make the world complete. "The LORD God said, It is not good that the man should be alone" (v. 18). The Lord then proceeded to create the woman from one of Adam's ribs (vv. 21–22). Having made her, the Lord brought her to the man (v. 22). This was the institution of marriage. It was the actual marrying of Adam and Eve, the first marriage. But it was also the institution of marriage as a lasting ordinance for the human race.

The original institution of marriage is basic for our understanding of marriage, our estimation of marriage, and our right behavior in marriage. It stands to reason that the instituting of marriage should be decisive regarding our view of marriage. For a proper understanding of anything, one needs to know its origin. How did it begin? What was its purpose originally? What characteristics did it then have?

Christ and his apostles explicitly teach the decisive significance of the institution of marriage on the sixth day of creation. When the Pharisees questioned him about divorce and, thus, about marriage, the Lord Jesus replied by referring back to the original institution of marriage. "And he answered and said unto them, Have ye not read, that he which made them at the beginning made them male and female" (Matt. 19:4). He then quoted Genesis 2:24 to the Pharisees. When the Pharisees pressed him with an appeal to the permission Moses gave to the Israelites to put their wives away, the Lord answered, "*From the beginning* it was not so" (Matt. 19:7–8; emphasis added). He demanded that, for the truth about marriage, and particularly for the truth about right behavior in marriage, we go back to the beginning, the institution of marriage. Paul does the same thing in 1 Timothy 2. In regard to the proper relationship between man and woman, the woman's subjection to the man, he finds proof for his teaching in the fact that originally "Adam was first formed, then Eve" (v. 13).

Accordingly, if we would properly estimate marriage and the duties of both persons in marriage, as well as the errors that threaten marriage, we must go back to the beginning: the institution of marriage by God.

The Incomplete Male

When on the sixth day of creation the man was by himself, he was incomplete; he was not whole. The Creator saw this: "It is not good that the man should be alone" (Gen. 2:18). The original Hebrew text expresses the unsatisfactory condition of the solitary man even more strongly. Literally, we read that God said, "It is not good for man to be in his separation." By himself Adam was living as one separated from someone else who belonged with him. There was a lack, and this was "not good."

In order to cause the man to experience this separation and incompleteness, God brings the animals to him. Adam, not having known any other condition, is not aware, as God is, that he is incomplete. By bringing the animals to Adam, God makes him aware of his lack. The animals are all paired off. Adam alone has no help meet for him. When we read in verse 20, "but for Adam there was not found an help meet for him," we must understand this as referring to Adam's own consciousness. Adam could not find a help meet for himself. Of course, he could not be definite yet as to the exact nature of his need. Only when God brings his complement to him will he know precisely what had been lacking. Yet, already now the sense of need is present.

It is necessary that Adam be aware of his incompleteness before God brings his wife to him. This will make a great difference in Adam's reception and treatment of the woman. Had Adam never realized his own incompleteness without her, he would have regarded the woman as a nice but really unnecessary addition to himself. He would have viewed her as dispensable. Now, however, he will receive her—and treat her—as one who is necessary for his own completion. He will know from experience that she is the help that he needs.

Marriage a Necessity

There is instruction in this regarding the necessity of marrying. God did not, after all, merely see that it was not good for man to be alone; he created man that way. He made Adam in such a way that by himself he was incomplete. It is increated in man that it is not good for him to remain unmarried. The same holds for the woman inasmuch as she was created not to be on her own but to be the help meet for the man. Therefore, it is practical wisdom to tell young men and young women of the church to marry.

There are exceptions. According to Matthew 19:12, some must be alone for the kingdom's sake: "There be eunuchs, which have made themselves eunuchs for the kingdom of heaven's sake."

God will give them grace so that they are able to live in this state. There are others who, like Paul, remain single for the sake of dedicating themselves to the work of the kingdom of Christ. Apart from the exceptions, however, the clear implication of God's creation of the man and the woman and his institution of marriage is that we ought to marry, always keeping in mind the proviso of Paul in 1 Corinthians 7:39: "only in the Lord."

The scriptures admonish the people of God to marry. 1 Corinthians 7:2 enjoins us, "Let every man have his own wife, and let every woman have her own husband." Paul states in 1 Timothy 5:14, "I will therefore that the younger women marry."

It is a grievous evil that the Roman Catholic Church requires her priests to live in separation. God says, "It is not good"; Rome says, "It is good." One cannot expect from this foolish and wicked law anything else than the corruptions of concubinage, fornication, homosexuality, and lust, which have resulted in the past, and which are still the results today.

Glorious Woman

Having prepared Adam to receive the woman as his wife, God created the woman. He first made Adam fall into a deep sleep; then from a rib which he took from the man, God made a woman. God bestowed the same high honor on the woman in his creation of her that he formerly gave to the man. First, before he created the woman, the Lord spoke concerning the creature he was about to make. He said, "It is not good that the man should be alone; I will make him an help meet for him" (Gen. 2:18). As was the case with the Lord's words prior to his creation of man in Genesis 1:26, this speech served to introduce a creature who would be the highest and most glorious of all creatures. Indeed, God's words in Genesis 1:26, "Let us make man in our image"—words that indicated the special significance of the creature, man—do not apply only to the male, but also to the female. The following verse shows this, for we read, "So God created man in his own image, in the image of God created he him; male and female created he them" (v. 27).

Second, the high honor of the woman is evident from the way in which God made her. He did not merely speak, calling her into existence by his word, but he worked on her with his own hands. Just as he formed man from the dust of the ground, so he took special pains with the woman and made her from a rib of Adam.

Literally, Genesis 2:22 says that the Lord "built" a woman from the rib of the man.

Apparent in God's creation of the woman is her lofty, glorious status. The woman has had a long history of being trampled on. This has especially been the case in heathen civilizations. She has differed little from the cattle that a man owned. Even in the church the notion has prevailed with some that the wife is a lowly creature, fit to bear whatever abuse the man might pour on her. Men have disdained their wives as if this were true piety, because the man is the head of his wife. Every such notion and practice is cut off simply by the account of the woman's creation in a position of high honor.

Help Meet

The honor accorded to the woman does not, however, detract from her creation as a "help meet" for the man. As used in the King James Version of the Bible, "meet" means suitable or fit.

We often misunderstand the phrase "help meet." God said that he would make "a help meet for Adam." A man shows that he fails to grasp what this means when he calls his wife a *helpmeet*, making the one word *helpmeet* out of the two words *help meet*. The woman is a help, an aid. She is a help, or aid, which is meet for the man; that is, she is just right for the man, fitted to him and his need. Adam, the man, is the standard. When God makes the woman, he makes her just what she should be to supply the lack of the man, just what she should be to complete him. She is the help of the man, suited for him in every respect, physically and bodily, but also mentally and emotionally. Therefore, she received the name *wo-man*. She is the female counterpart of the man. According to the original Hebrew, she is *ishshah*, for man is *ish*. Her name, expressing her very nature, is really *female man*.

A Divine Institution

God himself then brought the woman to Adam. So we read in Genesis 2:22: "and [God] brought her unto the man." This was the first marriage ceremony, solemnized by Jehovah God himself. This was the instituting of marriage as a permanent ordinance among men.

Marriage is an institution of God! The plain but fundamental truth about marriage is that God instituted it. The first marriage was a marriage that God made, from beginning to end. He willed it; he created the first two people in such a way that each was prepared for it, indeed, that neither could live without it; and he brought them together in the marriage bond. When God made this first marriage, he established a perpetual institution among men. On the sixth day God created marriage. He established an ordinance for all time, among all people.

The fundamental reason for man's corrupting of marriage is that he regards marriage not as a divine, but as a human institution.

The world, despising the authority of scripture, conceives another origin of marriage than that given in Genesis 2. Once upon a time (all fairy tales begin this way), man decided to make the institution of marriage. Man decided that marriage would be a useful ordinance for rearing a family and safeguarding his property. Because he did not want anyone to disturb his family life or jeopardize his property, man made some rules outlawing adultery.

This explanation of the origin of marriage is absolutely false. Adam had nothing to do with it; he did not even know marriage would be good for him until God revealed this to him. Once more—this time regarding the origin of marriage—there is the fundamental lie, in the beginning *man,* set over against the fundamental truth of Genesis 1:1, in the beginning *God.* Naturally, if marriage is a man-made institution, man may also do with that institution what he pleases. He may twist it and turn it to please himself and to suit his every whim and fancy. He may have mistresses. He may divorce for any reason and remarry. Western, nominally Christian civilization has degenerated to the point that it legalizes no-fault divorce. Divorce becomes as common—and as accepted—as marriage. If marriage is man's institution, man may overturn the institution. He may abolish it altogether if he pleases. This is what the radical youth are not only proposing, but doing. The less radical have "companionate" or trial marriages. The more radical repudiate marriage entirely and openly, unashamedly living in a state of fornication. Why not? Why not, if marriage is man-made? The parents and teachers of these youth may disapprove of their behavior, but if these parents and teachers deny that marriage is of divine institution, they cannot refute or rebuke the youth; in fact, they are responsible for the overturning of marriage by the youth. This destruction of marriage is the logical, inevitable result of the teaching of the state schools, where everything, including home and family, is man-centered and God-denying. To add at the end that marriage is good for society is too little, too late.

It is essential that we and our children see that marriage is an institution of the Lord God. We must see that it is not merely a human contract with mutual conditions and promises. But seeing this must be more than knowing it intellectually. For the time may come that the God of marriage makes a very hard demand of us. Then, although we know the truth of marriage with our minds, we are inclined to disregard the truth. We must, by the grace of the Holy Spirit, understand with a believing heart the truth that marriage is an institution of God. Our understanding must be filled with reverence for the God who instituted marriage. Then our attitude toward his institution of marriage will be one of fear and trembling. Above all, we must be motivated by deep, thankful love for him as the God of our salvation in Jesus Christ his Son. Out of such a motive, we ought humbly to hear his word on marriage and obediently follow it.

Because marriage is a divine institution, it is governed by God's regulations. The New Testament scriptures repeatedly direct us back to the beginning, back to God's original institution of marriage, for instruction in the laws governing marriage. They do so from the presupposition that God has the say-so concerning marriage.

Implied in this appeal to God's instituting of marriage is the fact that the principles of marriage are to be found in that original institution of marriage in the book of Genesis.

What are some of the principles of marriage—God's laws governing it—that are apparent in the institution of marriage in Genesis 2? First, "marriage is honourable in all, and the bed undefiled" (Heb. 13:4). It is the doctrine of devils to forbid marriage as something intrinsically vile (1 Tim. 4:1–3).

Second, marriage is the union and communion of one man and one woman. The limitation of one man and one woman in marriage is the law that our Lord points out, as evident in the institution of marriage in the beginning, in Matthew 19:3–12:

4. And he answered and said unto them, Have ye not read, that he which made them at the beginning made them male and female,

5. And said, For this cause shall a man leave father and mother, and shall cleave to his wife: and they twain shall be one flesh?

6. Wherefore they are no more twain, but one flesh. What therefore God hath joined together, let not man put asunder. (vv. 4–6)

According to this principle, there may be no divorce except for adultery and no remarriage as long as the man and his wife live.

Third, the man is the head in marriage, and the woman must be in submission to her husband. This is the conclusion that Paul, in 1 Corinthians 11, explicitly draws from the creation of Adam and Eve and from the original institution of marriage. In verse 3 he declares, "The head of the woman is the man." He bases this declaration on this: "the man is not of the woman; but the woman of the man. Neither was the man created for the woman; but the woman for the man" (vv. 8–9). The man was first, and the woman was second. The woman was made for the man, and not the man for the woman.

Fourth, the woman is necessary for the man; the man is incomplete without a wife. Paul goes on to elucidate this principle. He writes in verses 11–12: "Nevertheless neither is the man without the woman, neither the woman without the man, in the Lord. For as the woman is of the man, even so is the man also by the woman; but all things of God." That the woman had her origin out of man and for the sake of the man may not be high-mindedly misapplied by the man. Paul reminds the man that he is made in such a way that he cannot live "without the woman," but must live "by the woman." In accordance with Eve's creation from Adam, the wife lives her whole life out of her husband as the source; "the woman is of [out of] the man." But the husband, in keeping with Adam's completeness only after he received Eve, his wife, lives his whole life *through* the woman. His whole life—his life of thinking, of planning, and of working—passes through the woman, is affected by her, and is good, finally, because of her "help." Just as the woman may not live unsubmissively, the man may not live independently in relation to his wife, as if she were unnecessary to him and his life.

To fly in the face of these laws of marriage is to invite misery, even disaster. God punishes disobedient persons. But he punishes in such a way in this life that one's breaking of his laws is the very thing that brings a man into misery. When he disregards the laws of marriage, he steps off the path on which blessedness is enjoyed. He is like the foolish fish that decides to disregard the law that he live in the sphere of water, and he leaps to the ground. His action itself swiftly brings on him the misery due him. God's child enjoys the blessing of God in marriage as he learns and does God's will in marriage as an aspect of his thankfulness to God for gracious salvation in Jesus Christ.

A Creation Ordinance

In light of the account of God's institution of marriage, it is plain that marriage is an institution that belongs to the sphere of creation, not to the sphere of redemption. We should not misunderstand the truth that marriage is a symbol of the relationship between Christ and the church. This does not mean that marriage depends for its validity on the church or on God's grace. Marriage is not a sacrament, as Rome teaches. This would mean that marriage, like baptism, is instituted by Christ in the church and that it is a means of grace to the persons who participate. But God instituted marriage before there ever was any redemption or any church of Christ. Marriage is an ordinance of God in the realm of creation, similar to the ordinance of civil government and the ordinance of labor.

For this reason marriage is genuine outside the church, even as civil government is legitimate apart from the church. A marriage is valid before God and men, even though it was not solemnized by a minister. We condemn such a course of action by the youth of the church, but not because only that marriage is valid which is performed in the church. Unbelievers are validly married, just as they are genuinely possessors and wielders of the authority of civil government. Therefore, those unbelievers who commit adultery are judged and condemned by God for a real violation of a true marriage.

But the unbeliever does not honor marriage as the institution of God, nor does he honor it as the mystery of Christ and the church. Even when he formally conforms to God's laws for marriage, he does not do so to the glory of God. He ends, in his marriage too, in himself. Therefore, he sins in his marriage from beginning to end. Because the unbeliever does not regard God's word in the matter of his marriage, he is ignorant of the true wisdom concerning marriage and therefore foolishly plunges himself into many miseries. Refusing to honor marriage as God's institution, he throws open the door to the corruption and destruction of marriage. Only the regenerated child of God can honor marriage. He honors it by receiving it from God as God's institution. He honors it by living in it according to God's laws. Thus he displays in the reality of his married life the living relationship of love between Jesus Christ and the church.

3

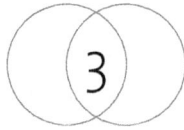

The Christian Man as Husband

Likewise, ye husbands, dwell with them according to knowledge, giving honour unto the wife, as unto the weaker vessel, and as being heirs together of the grace of life; that your prayers be not hindered. —1 Peter 3:7

How Christian men behave toward their wives is nothing less than a test of their faith in Jesus Christ. A man may make a sound, and even profound profession of his faith, but if he abuses his wife, he gives the lie to that profession. A man's wife is his neighbor, his nearest neighbor. This neighbor, because she is nearest him, he is to love above all others. If a man refuses to love his wife, whom he has seen, how can he love God, whom he has not seen? Such a man should be interrupted in the middle of his profound profession of faith and told, Go home, and begin to love your wife!

The attitude and behavior of the Christian man toward his wife are also important in the eyes of the world. When the unbelieving world sees a confessing Christian, a member of the church, mistreat his wife, they doubt his confession, conclude that membership in the church is of no real significance, and come, finally, to reproach the Christ whom that man confesses with his mouth. That man is to blame for this. He has given the world occasion to reproach the church and her head. Likewise, when the institution of marriage is openly and widely corrupted, as at the present time, the godly behavior of Christian husbands toward their wives is an effective and beautiful testimony of the Lord Jesus. This can serve as an additional incentive for heeding the calling of 1 Peter 3:7, the calling of the Christian man as husband.

That the Holy Spirit confronts the husband with a certain calling regarding marriage makes plain that the husband is not autonomous in marriage. This is a mistake the man tends to make. He notes that the woman is subject to his authority, as the first six verses of 1 Peter 3 teach. He notes also that he is the head of his wife, even the lord, as 1 Peter 3:6 states. From this the man concludes that his will is sovereign in his marriage. This conclusion is refuted by the very fact that scripture, here and elsewhere, lays down requirements for the man in marriage. Husbands, dwell with your wives and give honor to them, the text says. Not the will of the husband, but the will of another, who is over the husband, is sovereign in marriage.

The same thing is brought out by the word with which 1 Peter 3:7 begins: "likewise." This word refers back to 1 Peter 2:13, where the apostle writes, "Submit yourselves to every ordinance of man for the Lord's sake." There are certain human ordinances that the Lord has established in the creation.

The Christian is called to submit to these "for the Lord's sake." One of these ordinances is civil government. The Christian citizen submits to it by subjecting himself to the authority of the ruler. Another ordinance is labor. The Christian employee submits to it by being in subjection to his "master," his employer, the froward as well as the good and gentle (1 Pet. 2:18). Marriage is another such ordinance of God. The Christian woman submits to it by being in subjection to her husband (1 Pet. 3:1).

But the Christian man must also submit to the ordinance of marriage. His position in marriage is, from this viewpoint, the same as that of his wife: submission. *"Likewise,* ye husbands" (emphasis added), says the Holy Spirit; that is, "You also are called to submit yourselves in this matter of marriage. You are not sovereigns here, to do as you please." The husband, however, submits to the Lord. He does this by carrying out the calling the Lord gives him.

There are three aspects of this calling of the Christian man as husband. He is called to dwell with his wife; he is called to be understanding toward his wife; and he is called to bless his wife.

Masculine Independency

An error into which the Christian husband may fall is that of regarding himself as basically independent of his wife. Naturally enough, he tends to live independently. He has his own ambitions, his own interests, his own entertainments, and he pursues them by himself. His wife is not brought into this life of his but, in fact, is shut out. Inevitably, this independence becomes a cause of friction in the marriage. It may even lead to actual separation. Then the husband is usually surprised, even indignant. He never was cruel. He always took good care of her and the children financially. He cannot understand why his wife feels as bitter or hopeless as she does and why the marriage is "on the rocks." But the cause is his independent life.

There are symptoms of this evil on the part of the husband. He is seldom at home. Evenings and weekends he is gone, by himself, on matters of interest to himself. If he is at home, he does not commune with his wife, whether about matters of his own personal life or about their mutual concerns; he is wrapped up in his own thoughts and activities. The trouble with him is that he has the notion that he is independent in his marriage.

Perhaps the husband even bases this independency on the original institution of marriage. Was not the man created first and the woman second? Was not Eve made for Adam, to be a help meet for him? And does this not imply that the man pretty much goes his own way in life while the wife must content herself with helping him when she can? After all, the man is not intended to be the help of the woman. Even if our thinking is not quite as crude as this, we husbands do well to examine ourselves to see whether this is our idea of marriage. If it is, we are disobedient to our calling from the Lord. We are not submissive to the ordinance of marriage. We do not behave ourselves as Christian men. If this is our thinking and behavior, we do not reflect the heavenly bridegroom, Jesus Christ, but horribly misrepresent him. Nor can we expect very much from our marriages. They will not be joyful realities for us, and they will not be relationships that manifest the mystery of Christ and the church.

Over against this notion of the man's independence stands the institution of marriage. The husband bent on being independent appeals to the institution, but erroneously. The man was indeed created by God as the head of his wife; the wife was indeed made as a help for him. What is forgotten is that the wife was made as a help for the man because without her the man was incomplete. Adam was not self-sufficient. He needed the woman. There is, therefore, a dependency of the man upon his wife. For a husband to assert his independency is for him stupidly to blunder along in disregard for the fact that for the man to be alone is not good.

Scripture expressly warns the husband against viewing his headship as independency. In 1 Corinthians 11, after insisting that "the head of the woman is the man" (v. 3), Paul adds, "Nevertheless neither is the man without the woman, neither the woman without the man, in the Lord. For as the woman is of the man, even so is the man also by the woman; but all things of God" (vv. 11–12). The man does not live apart from the woman in independency; he lives "*by* the woman" (emphasis added), that is, *through* her. The institution of marriage consisted of this: God made the man and his wife one flesh. They have one life. Independence on the man's part is revolution against the ordinance of marriage.

This independence is also contrary to the great standard for the Christian man in his life as husband. That great standard is the attitude and behavior of Jesus Christ toward the church. Marriage is the mystery of Christ and the church. Christ Jesus does not live apart from the church, his wife, in independency. That which makes this all the more compelling for the Christian husband is the fact that Jesus did not need the church. As the eternal Son of God, Christ was completely self-sufficient. Of him it could never be said that it was not good for him to be alone. But in free grace he united himself to the church and lives with that church and through that church forever. He lives with the church! He shares his life with her. He communes with her about his secret thoughts, his desires and plans, and all his activities. He keeps nothing from her. He brings her into his life, fully. This now is the pattern for the Christian man as husband. This is why the Christian husband has the calling in 1 Peter 3:7: "Likewise, ye husbands, dwell with them." It is a calling that condemns and prohibits all independency.

The calling to dwell with one's wife should be understood, first, in the literal, even physical sense. First Corinthians 7:3

commands husbands and wives to live with each other sexually: "Let the husband render unto the wife due benevolence: and likewise also the wife unto the husband." "Due benevolence" describes a debt that each owes the other so that the apostle admonishes husbands and wives to pay the debt. The reference is to the sexual relationship and act, as the context makes unmistakably plain. It may seem strange that this is made a command, yet it has happened that married persons renounced sex more fully to consecrate themselves to God. Today as well, the refusal of husband or wife, probably not for a spiritual reason, poses a threat to marriage.

The calling of the husband to dwell with his wife also means that he be at home with his wife. In the world worthless husbands hang out in taverns. The Christian husband may sin similarly by finding many activities, perhaps recreational, that keep him away from home. When he is at home, he must live there in fellowship with his wife and must not merely exist under the same roof with her. Thus the calling takes on the broadest possible significance, requiring the husband to share his entire life with his wife. He must live his life *through* her.

Male Tyranny

Just as the calling to dwell with one's wife prohibits independency, so it also forbids tyranny. This is another prevalent, un-Christian characteristic of husbands. In this case the husband rules his wife in an absolutely cold and cruel manner. The nature of this "reign of terror" is such that it is devoid of love. It is exclusively a matter of sheer power. The nature of the rule of the husband is that the man uses his wife; he pleases and enhances himself at his wife's expense. He is a tyrant. This is the lordship of the sinful, unbelieving husband. This kind of rule by the husband was the judgment God imposed on the woman in paradise because of her guilt in the fall. We read of this in Genesis 3:16: "Unto the woman he said, I will greatly multiply thy sorrow and thy conception; in sorrow thou shalt bring forth children; and thy desire shall be to thy husband, and he shall rule over thee." The judgment is that her husband will rule over her. But there was a rule by the husband already before the fall. The man was vested with authority over the woman by virtue of creation. The rule, therefore, that Genesis 3:16 speaks of, and that first comes about after the fall, is the brutal, tyrannical rule over the weaker, submitting female by the stronger, domineering male. But this is certainly not the standard for the Christian man. This is not the pious behavior called for by 1 Peter 3:7.

We may not deny the headship and authority of the Christian husband. Peter insists on it, for he refers to the wife as "the weaker vessel." Also, the preceding verses require the wife to be in subjection to her husband, having Sarah as her model, who obeyed Abraham and called him "lord." The pattern for this headship is the behavior of Jesus Christ toward the church, of which he is the head. The headship of Jesus toward the church makes plain that it is the essential calling of the husband to *love* his wife. The basic calling is not rule your wife, as if you were a dictator, but the calling is love her because you are her husband. This love is not a grasping, self-seeking love, but a giving love. "Husbands, love your wives, even as Christ also loved the church," Ephesians 5:25 requires and then adds, "and gave himself for it." That Jesus is the head of the church does not mean that he uses her for his own advantage, but that he gives himself for her benefit. In love he *gave!* In love he gave *himself.* In like manner the husband should love his wife. In the context of such love, let the husband exercise his headship and authority.

In a time of marital trouble, the husband often complains that the cause is the disobedience of his wife. He will loudly insist, "I am the head; I rule." It may be necessary to reply, "Yes, but do you dwell with her? Is this basic relationship present between you and her? Is there communion of life between you and your wife because you love her and give yourself for her?" This is the fundamental element in our relationship with Jesus Christ: communion of life, covenantal fellowship in love. This is also the fundamental element in marriage, which is patterned after "the things in the heavenlies." Therefore, Peter does not say, "Husbands, rule over your wives." But he says, "Husbands, *live with* your wives." A head, disconnected from the body, trying still to dominate that body, is a monstrosity. The head can only rule the body in and through its intimate connection with the body. This is true of our physical bodies; this is true of Christ and the church; this is also true of man and wife.

The Knowledge of Love

These evils that threaten the life of the Christian man as husband are warded off by the requirement of knowledge: "Ye husbands, dwell with them according to knowledge" (1 Pet. 3:7). Knowledge on the part of the husband is to be the standard according to which he lives with his wife. This knowledge is not a knowledge only of the mind—a cold, abstract head knowledge. Rather, it is the warm, personal knowledge of the heart. The exhortation in 1 Peter comes close to this: be an understanding man! The knowledge required is a sympathetic knowledge. In keeping with the usual significance of knowledge in the Bible, the core of this knowledge is love.

This knowledge is a spiritual gift to the Christian husband by the Holy Spirit. It is not a natural affection or feeling. It is not a natural characteristic that some men are born with. I stress this because, especially in a time of severe trouble in marriage, a husband may have this idea about the knowledge that is required of him, so that he either excuses his sins of not living with his wife according to knowledge or concludes that his marriage is hopeless. He will say, "It is not my nature to be understanding or patient; I am rough and firm." What he means is, "My harsh behavior and thoughtlessness toward my wife in the past is something that could not be helped, something for which I really cannot be blamed."

Or this may be the expression of despair concerning the future: "I would like to live with my wife in the right way, but I fear the weakness and sinfulness of my nature." The wife makes the same mistake if she supposes that love is merely a natural feeling. If then she should lose the feeling of affection for her husband, she will either conclude that she has the right to break up the marriage or that the future of her marriage is dismal and hopeless.

The virtues required of us as husbands and wives are not natural characteristics that one either possesses or lacks from birth. They are not earthly feelings that we have to drum up in ourselves. They are divine gifts. Love is Christ's love shed abroad in our hearts by the Holy Spirit, as we beseech it in prayer. A marriage is not hopeless, therefore, even though the feeling of affection has disappeared through our sin. Thoughtful, understanding, sympathetic knowledge is not something that some men are born with, but it is a heavenly gift of Christ to believing men who ask for it daily in prayer. Hence it is possible for every Christian man to have it and exercise it. It is his sin if he does not.

Weaker Vessel

The knowledge that must be the standard according to which the husband dwells with his wife is also intellectual. It knows certain things about the wife and thus enables the man to take these things into account when he lives with her. There is one characteristic of the wife in particular which the text requires the husband always to take into account. This is that the wife is a weaker vessel. The translation of the King James Version is incorrect here. It reads: "dwell with them according to knowledge, giving honour unto the wife, as unto the weaker vessel, and as being heirs together of the grace of life" (1 Pet. 3:7). The correct translation is "dwell with them according to knowledge as with the weaker vessel, the female, giving them honor as to those who are coheirs of the grace of life." This translation makes clear that the husband's knowledge of his wife concerns her status and condition as a "weaker vessel."

Here is God's denial of the wife's equality with her husband. The unbelieving wife mocks at this teaching of holy scripture and hates it in her heart. She will never yield to it. But the believer, accepting this teaching of the inequality of husband and wife as God's word, is concerned to know its meaning.

What does it mean that the wife is the weaker vessel? The correct translation of the text makes clear what Peter means: "dwell with them according to knowledge as with the weaker vessel, the female." The wife is the weaker vessel because she is a woman, not a man; a female, not a male. Peter refers to the subordination of the woman to the man that God established in his creation of these two creatures. For this reason, the woman ought never to regard her relative weakness as shameful. The moon might as well suppose itself to be dishonorable because it is dependent on the sun. Every creature of God was made with its own glory. It is part of the glory of the female that she is the weaker vessel.

From the beginning the status of the female was one of subordination to the male, for the Creator made her *after* the man, *according to* the man's need, and *for the sake of the* man. This was the case exactly because God willed the woman's position in marriage to be submission, dependence, and help. God created the woman in such a way that her nature, her make-up, reflected and made possible her subordinate position in marriage. He made her weaker than the man. She is weaker in the strength of the body. She is also weaker in the strength of the soul; that is, the intellect, the will, and the emotions. The outrage of the advocates of women's liberation does not change this. For this is a "law" of creation. Her relative weakness is increated in the woman's nature. The attack upon this law of God in creation is part of the antichrist's heaven-storming defiance in the last days, according to which he "think[s] to change times and laws" (Dan. 7:25).

It is true that sin has affected also this aspect of creation so that some men are weaker than some women, not only mentally and emotionally but also physically. But this does not contradict the truth of the apostle's general assertion that the female is weaker than the male, for the apostle speaks of the woman's place in marriage, of her relationship to the man in marriage. She is the weaker vessel in marriage, and he is the stronger. This does not mean that the husband is always more brilliant intellectually or more stable emotionally, but that the wife, by virtue of being a woman, depends on her husband with her entire nature, body, and soul.

Having knowledge of this, the husband will treat his wife with kindness. He will be careful in his behavior toward her so that he does not injure or break the weaker vessel. The weakness of the woman which incites the unbelieving husband to brutality must incline the Christian man to tender consideration. Because of his wife's weakness, he will nourish and cherish her. This is how Christ treats his wife, the weaker vessel, the church, as Paul writes in Ephesians 5:29.

The danger is that the man's knowledge that his wife is the weaker vessel may become contempt for her. Especially when the husband experiences the weakness of his wife, when her dependency annoys him, when she irritates or disappoints him, he is tempted to allow his knowledge of her weakness to turn into contempt. First Peter 3:7 guards against this perversion of the husband's knowledge of the wife as the weaker vessel when it adds, in the words of the more accurate translation, "giving them honor as to those who are coheirs of the grace of life."

First, the husband is warned against all arrogance and contempt by the reminder that he too is but a *vessel*. The wife is the "weaker vessel," which implies that the husband is the stronger vessel. But he is only a vessel: like his wife a creature of clay, not the Potter.

Second, the husband is and must know himself to be an heir of the grace of life. This is implied when the text calls wives "heirs together," or "coheirs," of the grace of life. They are heirs together with their husbands. There is a reason why the Spirit at this point reminds the husband that he is an heir of the grace of life. The Christian man must live with his wife, standing always beneath the tree of Golgotha, conscious always of God's pure grace and great mercy to him. Consequently, he cannot treat his wife contemptuously.

The third consideration that prevents the husband from holding his wife in contempt and that demands that he honor her is the point that Peter expressly makes in the text: she is also an heir of the grace of life. One's wife, as a believer, is a child of God, a recipient of God's marvelous grace and an heir of God's own life and glory. From this viewpoint she is the equal of her husband. There is no difference between the believing man and the believing woman. There is neither male nor female, but both are one in Christ (Gal. 3:28). As an heir of life, the woman is precious to

Jesus Christ. Not only may her husband not despise her, but he must also hold her in high esteem as a daughter of God and show this esteem in his conduct.

The text has touched here on the spiritual oneness of the Christian man and the Christian woman in marriage. It has in mind a marriage in which both the husband and the wife are heirs of the grace of eternal life. Therefore, the text also speaks of the prayers of both the man and his wife, which must not be hindered. God requires believers to marry believers, and he forbids marriage with an unbeliever. Marry "only in the Lord," writes Paul in 1 Corinthians 7:39. The intimacy of a Christian marriage is the oneness of the husband and his wife in the Lord Jesus Christ. As one flesh, they not only share one natural life, but they also share one spiritual life. And this shared spiritual life is at the center of the natural, earthly life they have in common. Their spiritual unity enables them to be one in the living of their earthly life.

Sharing the spiritual life of Christ through the Spirit is the essence of the fellowship of the Christian marriage. Because of this the Christian man and his Christian wife realize to the fullest God's purpose with the institution of marriage. Also before the fall, the intimate fellowship of Adam and Eve in marriage was grounded in their perfect fellowship with God. They were married, not apart from God but in God. Therefore, when they separated themselves from God, they also became estranged from each other. Fallen Eve was willing to ruin her husband and hence tempted him to sin. Fallen Adam was willing to have his wife destroyed and hence laid the blame for the fall upon her.

Headship as Responsibility

In Christ the believing husband and wife share one spiritual life, so closely are they brought together in marriage. This implies a certain weighty responsibility for the husband. He is called to be the head of his wife also with regard to their spiritual life. He bears a responsibility for his wife's spiritual well-being. God calls him to bless his wife. This does not mean that the husband has the power to save his wife. Only Jesus Christ can efficaciously bless and save people. But Jesus does use the Christian husband for the spiritual welfare of his believing wife. She, on her part, leans on her husband in spiritual things. Paul points to this in 1 Corinthians 14:35: "and if they will learn any thing, let them ask their husbands at home."

The great standard is the relationship between Jesus and his church: "For the husband is the head of the wife, even as Christ is the head of the church: and he is the saviour of the body" (Eph. 5:23). Christ is the savior of the church. This is reflected in the Christian marriage, when the husband is the spiritual leader, when he gives firm guidance to his wife and family, when he teaches his wife the truth of God, and when he leads in prayer and in the study of the scriptures. A husband may well ask himself, do I do this? Am I able to do this? It is a sad thing when a husband abdicates this office and forces his wife to be the spiritual power in the marriage and home. It is even worse when he corrupts this office and leads his wife and children away from Christ.

But a husband may be responsible for weakening his wife's spiritual condition and tearing down the spiritual life they share, even though he leads in prayer at the table, takes his wife to church, and teaches her. He does this by his bad behavior as a husband. This is what the text means when it adds, "that your prayers be not hindered." This is to be the purpose of the Christian husband as he obeys the calling given to him in the text. The implication is that if he does not dwell with his wife, if he does not thoughtfully take into account that she is the weaker vessel, and if he does not give her honor as a coheir of eternal life, their prayers will be hindered. Not only will his personal prayers to God be hindered, but also the prayers that he and his wife pray together, prayers on behalf of their marriage, prayers on behalf of their children, and prayers on behalf of the one calling they have from God to glorify him in their marriage. When their prayers stop, their marriage deteriorates, for the marriage is blessed by God only as they pray for that blessing. The fellowship becomes strained, and all kinds of troubles arise. All of this is due to the sin of the husband who refuses to carry out his calling of dwelling with his wife according to knowledge.

This is our experience, is it not? When for a time we husbands live independently, or play the tyrant, or simply live thoughtlessly in our relationship with our wives, we find that God cuts our prayers off. When we try to come to the throne of grace, he says, "Man, go first to your wife; confess your sins to her; begin once more to live with her according to knowledge." We find that we and our wives cannot pray together, so that our marriages become a great misery instead of a great joy. This is the reason the Christian man repents and converts himself. He finds this situation intolerable. It is intolerable that he cannot pray. It is intolerable that he is estranged from his own flesh. It is intolerable that his marriage fails brilliantly to reflect the intimacy of Christ and the church.

What a lofty position is ours, who are Christian husbands! What an important calling is ours! It is worthy of our greatest efforts. We ought to work, and work hard, at this calling. Let us turn daily to our Lord Jesus Christ for the strength. The power to carry out this calling is in him. In him we can do all things, including the calling of the Christian husband.

4

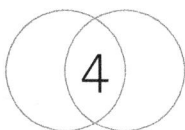

The Christian Woman as Wife

That they may teach the young women to be sober, to love their husbands, to love their children, To be discreet, chaste, keepers at home, good, obedient to their own husbands, that the word of God be not blasphemed. —Titus 2:4–5

It is the duty of the older women in the church to instruct the younger women in their calling as wives. Titus 2:4–5 sets forth the calling of the young married women. But it is not the minister, Titus, who is to teach this to the young women directly. The minister must speak the things which become sound doctrine (v. 1). He must speak to the older women (v. 3), so that they in turn will teach the younger married women. The older women of the church, whether married or unmarried, have a definite responsibility to the younger women, a certain "office" to fulfill. There is good reason for this. The older women are able to do what the minister or the elder, as a man, is not as capable of doing. Naturally enough, the young women rely on the older women. They go to the older women with their questions and problems, so that the older women have the opportunity to instruct the young women. This is especially true of the older women who are mothers in Israel and who are, therefore, looked to by their daughters and daughters-in-law. They must make use of these opportunities to teach the young women to be sober, to love their husbands, to love their children, and to do all of the other duties of the text.

But the older women do not teach only by words. They are also called to teach by their example. The young wives see in the behavior of the older women a pattern that they should follow, especially in the behavior of their mothers. It is particularly the behavior of the older women toward their husbands that is an influential example for the young women. The example that mothers give to their daughters is most effective instruction, whether for good or bad. From their earliest years, daughters should grow up in a home in which their mother's relationship to their father is the godly one set forth in Titus 2:4–5. By means of their lives the older women, especially mothers, must be "teachers of good things" (v. 3).

Although the viewpoint is that of the calling of the older women to teach the younger, the text presents a complete description of the Christian young woman as wife. Our reaction to the young wife pictured here is, "What a beautiful and noble creature she is." She is glorious with the same glory that shines in the wife of Proverbs 31. She differs from the women of the world as beauty differs from ugliness and as nobility differs from baseness. Hers is genuine beauty and true adornment: "a meek and quiet spirit," as Peter says, "which is in the sight of God of great price" (1 Pet. 3:4). "Her children arise up, and call her blessed; her husband also, and he praiseth her" (Prov. 31:28).

We find that her beauty and glory consist of three main virtues. She is obedient; she is sound-minded, or, as the text in Titus puts it, "sober" and "discreet"; she is God-fearing. This is the calling of every Christian woman as wife.

Submission

When one reads all of the passages in the New Testament that give the calling of the wife in marriage, he discovers that the fundamental calling is subjection to her husband. It is striking that the wife is only rarely told to love her husband. Over and over, the wife is called to be in subjection and to obey. The text in Titus is one of the few passages that mention the wife's love for her husband. The explanation for this is not, of course, the insignificance of the wife's love. Rather, the explanation is the tremendous importance of submission and obedience.

First, consider several of the outstanding New Testament passages on the calling of the wife. Ephesians 5:22–33 admonishes, "Wives, submit yourselves unto your own husbands...As the church is subject unto Christ, so let the wives be to their own husbands in every thing...[Let] the wife see that she reverence her husband." Colossians 3:18 exhorts, "Wives, submit yourselves unto your own husbands, as it is fit in the Lord." First Peter 3:1–6 contains the following instruction: "Ye wives, be in subjection to your own husbands;...the holy women also, who trusted in God, adorned themselves, being in subjection unto their own husbands: Even as Sara obeyed Abraham, calling him lord." First Corinthians 11:3 says that "the head of the woman is the man." First Timothy 2:12 forbids the woman "to usurp authority over the man."

There can be no question that God calls the wife to be in subjection to her husband and to obey, and that this is the basic calling of the wife. If this is present in her, the wife can also do the other things required of her. If this is lacking, she must fail in all the other aspects of her wifely calling also. If she is not in subjection, neither will she be sober, a lover of her husband and children, or good. For the wife, the virtue of subjection is crucial.

Paul mentions this virtue in Titus 2:5: "obedient to their own husbands." The word that is translated as "obedient" is the word that elsewhere in scripture is translated as "be in subjection," or "be submissive." The literal reading of verse 5 would be: "submissive to their own husbands."

There is a distinction between being submissive and obeying. First, they are two different words in the Bible. Both are found together in 1 Peter 3:5–6: "The holy women also, who trusted in God, adorned themselves, *being in subjection* unto their own husbands: Even as Sara *obeyed* Abraham [emphasis added]."

The holy women in the Old Testament were in subjection, and they obeyed.

Second, these two different words have their own distinct meaning. Being in subjection refers to the inner attitude of a wife's heart, according to which she knows her husband to be in authority over her and freely wills it. Subjection, or submission, is altogether invisible and secret. It is a matter of the heart, as is everything important. This is what Peter calls "the hidden man of the heart..., a meek and quiet spirit" (1 Pet. 3:4). Within—in her heart—the submissive wife consciously, actively places herself under the authority of the husband regarding her person and her entire life. Obedience, in distinction from submission, refers to one's outward behavior. The obedient wife does what her husband tells her to do. But she does more than this. She lives her entire life in conformity with her husband's will.

Submission and obedience are related. Submission in the heart is the source and cause of obedience; obedience is the fruit and manifestation of submission. If a wife is in subjection to her husband, she will obey him. If a wife is disobedient to her husband, it is because she does not submit in her heart. The relationship is shown in 1 Peter 3:4–5. Holy women of the past were in subjection to their husbands; therefore, like Sara, they obeyed their husbands.

Submission is basic. Therefore, although it also requires obedience, scripture stresses the calling of the wife to be in subjection. This is literally what Titus 2:5 says: the young women must be in subjection to their husbands. This calling is absolute and unqualified. There are no exceptions. There are no circumstances that permit a wife to disregard this calling.

Ephesians 5:24 is plain: "As the church is subject unto Christ, so let the wives be to their own husbands in every thing." When the Holy Spirit requires the wife to submit in everything, he not only refers to those things that belong to the mutual life of the husband and wife (their relationship, the running of the home, and the upbringing of the children), but he also includes everything that belongs to the wife's personal life.

Implied is the command that the wife be in subjection always. She must be in subjection when her husband lives with her according to knowledge, as he is required to do. But she must be in subjection also when he fails to do his calling and manifests himself as self-centered and harsh. Even when the wife cannot and may not obey, she can and must be in subjection. Nowhere does God require the woman to obey in everything. A husband might order his wife to sin, especially if the husband is an unbeliever. Even a believing husband might order an unreasonable, harmful, or evil action on the part of his wife. In such cases the wife does not obey. But she still is in subjection. This will be evident in her demeanor as she disobeys. She does not disobey as a rebel, but meekly.

Rebellion

Wives can sin against the commandment of submission in two ways. A wife may be an out-and-out rebel against the lordship of her husband. She opposes and contradicts him. She disobeys and overrules him. The result is hellish confusion and warfare in the home, for the home now has two heads. There is no order, only chaos. If a woman persists in this rebellion, the warning of Romans 13:2 applies to her: "Whosoever therefore resisteth the power, resisteth the ordinance of God: and they that resist shall receive to themselves damnation."

Another form of disobedience to the calling of the wife is the wife's ignoring her husband and independently living her life as she pleases. This is what the apostle refers to in 1 Timothy 2:12, when he speaks of the woman's usurping authority over the man. In this case the wife is simply not under the authority of her husband. She is a law to herself and goes her own way. She refuses to live her life "out of the man" (1 Cor. 11:12). She does not seek to please the man, as 1 Corinthians 7:34 teaches: "She that is married careth for the things of the world, how she may please her husband." She does not live as a help to her husband—this and this only—but as an independent person seeking her own things.

In both cases the wife shows willful disregard for marriage as a divine institution, for the ground of the calling of the wife to submit and obey is God's original institution of marriage. In the beginning God created the man first and the woman second. He made the woman for the man, to be a help meet for him, not to be an independent person alongside of him.

Added to this ground of wifely submission is the fact that the woman first fell into sin. This is taught by Paul in 1 Timothy 2:14. As another reason the woman must not usurp authority over the man, he says, "And Adam was not deceived, but the woman being deceived was in the transgression." Paul's reference to the role of the woman in the fall is fitting in the context of instruction concerning the woman's duty to be in subjection to the man. In the fall the wife erred in presenting herself as an independent power alongside her husband. She did this by carrying on a discussion with the serpent about God's prohibition of eating from the tree of knowledge. She should not have engaged in the discussion. God had given the man the commandment regarding the tree, not the woman. Genesis 3:2 should have read, "See my husband, serpent; he is my head, and I live only under him and out of him." Adam also erred by permitting his wife to get away with her usurpation of his authority. But God insisted on his ordinance: the authority of the man in marriage. For he came into the garden asking, "Adam, where are you?" He did not ask, "Eve, where are you?"

God gave the husband authority in the marriage bond, and God put the wife under that authority. *God did!* And still today, God maintains the original institution. *God does!* The wife is under her husband's authority. She is not a ruling head, but an obeying body. She is this whether she likes it or not, whether she lives that way or not. The calling of the Christian woman as wife is to honor the institution of marriage. Consciously, willingly agree to it; occupy that position; live that way. This is pleasing to God: not so much that you call your husband "honey" or "sweetheart," but that you call him "lord."

Spiritual Sanity

Basic to the willingness of a wife to be in subjection to her husband is a sound mind. In the text in Titus, Paul twice uses the word that means "sound-minded." They are the words translated as "sober" and "discreet." The young wives must be sober and discreet, that is, sound-minded. The idea is that if the young wife has a sound mind, she will submit to her husband and obey him, whereas if she entertains foolish thoughts, she will not submit.

The young wife is tempted to think foolishly about marriage, particularly about her calling in marriage, by the example of the unbelieving wives of the world. These women reject the fundamental virtue of the wife: submission. Especially in our time and in our society, they deny it and ridicule it. They claim that the wife is an equal partner in marriage. They insist that marriage is a contract between equals. There is, they say, no authority in this relationship, only mutual agreement. Also, they view the wife as basically independent of her husband. Although married, she has her own life, her own career, her own fulfillment as a woman, apart from her husband. In short, she is not and must not be considered to be a help meet for her husband.

These damnable lies have pernicious results. They are directly responsible for the appalling increase in broken marriages and homes, with all of the attendant misery and woe. No home that has two heads, or no head at all, can stand. Besides, where the authority of the husband over the wife is lacking, the authority of the parents over the children will invariably be lacking also so that lawless parents spawn lawless children. These bitter consequences of the wife's rejection of her husband's authority are nothing else than God's judgment on those who despise his ordinance of marriage.

The example of the world is not the only temptation to the Christian wife. She has a sinful nature that is opposed to the calling to submit to her husband; by nature she is a rebel. According to her nature she does not will to be in subjection to another, but to assert herself. She does not will to be the help of another, but to seek herself.

Over against the example of the world and over against your

own nature now, be of a sound mind, says Paul. What is this sound mind? Essentially, it is the thinking of the young wife that considers how the church, the bride, is related to Christ, her husband, and how that church conducts herself toward Christ. Then, it is the thinking that applies this great truth to her marriage and to her calling in marriage. Marriage is the mystery of Christ and the church. Thus to regard marriage is to have a sound mind, that is, to be sober and discreet. Just as the church submits to and obeys her head, Jesus Christ, so you are to submit to your husband and obey him. The church submits in everything. Nothing of her life falls outside the sphere of his authority. And the church obeys Christ even though the Lord requires hard things of her. Obedience to Christ often means loss, hardship, and even death for the church. Nor does the church live her life or any part of her life apart from Christ, in independence of him. She has no life except her life in Christ. So the life of the Christian wife should be.

This is not some great evil for the church. This is the blessedness, the true happiness of the church. In the way of complete submission to Christ and in the way of living in him, with him, and out of him, the church is blessed in time and eternity. So it is for the Christian wife. When God calls her to submit, he points out the way of happiness and life for her.

Young Christian wives must also be of a sound mind in their view of other important aspects of marriage. The text mentions them: their love for their own husbands, their love for their children, and their being "keepers at home." The Holy Spirit makes plain here that love is an essential element in the wife's calling. She must love her husband. The reason scripture stresses submission so strongly is not that scripture minimizes love. In fact, the first and great commandment to the young wife is: love your husband. Love is the fundamental virtue in marriage, also concerning the calling of the wife. Submission and obedience are the form that love takes in the case of the wife, the way that her love manifests itself. There can be no question about this in light of the great pattern of marriage. The basic characteristic of the relationship of the church to Christ is that the church loves Christ. In her love she submits and obeys. Scripture does not minimize the importance of the wife's love, but it is concerned that this love will be genuine and that it will express itself and take form properly. And that form is submission!

Romance and Realism

In close connection with this concern, scripture guards against a false romanticism concerning marriage to which young women are prone. Young women are inclined to dream of marriage as all emotional, passionate love, as a matter of moonlit nights and idyllic days. With such fantasies they enter marriage. When they wake up to reality, they quickly desert their husbands and divorce. This is the view of marriage peddled by the world in its novels, movies, and television. In contrast scripture displays a matter-of-factness, a sober realism, about marriage that the Christian young woman should incorporate into her thinking before marriage and retain throughout her marriage. Not that scripture destroys her idealism concerning marriage or is a foe of romance. Have you never read the Song of Solomon? The estimation of marriage that regards it as nothing less than the mystery of Christ and the church insists on the highest idealism and opens the way to romance for every Christian marriage.

But the word of God gives the young women of the church the whole truth so they can have a sound mind. In marriage they can expect children, the bearing and rearing of whom will mean pain and sorrow. They must expect to be "keepers at home," or as a better translation has it, "workers at home." Theirs is not the glamour of the career woman, but the patient, unsung, and often wearisome labor of the home and family. Even their love of their husband will not be an emotional, passionate, spontaneous thing, at least not entirely this, for the text teaches that this love for the husband is *taught* to the young wives by the older women. The aged women must "teach the young women to be sober, to love their husbands" (v. 4). If the older women teach this love, the young wives must learn this love. This is arduous, spiritual activity, for the husband, although a Christian, will soon prove himself to be no "prince charming," but a very weak and sinful man, whom it is not always easy to love.

Spiritual Madness

If these characteristics of a wife are the product of a sound mind, it is evident that the world is mad. The women of the world in our day are fools, diseased of mind, walking "in the vanity of their mind, having the understanding darkened, being alienated from the life of God through the ignorance that is in them, because of the blindness of their heart," as Paul says in Ephesians 4:17–18. For they do the very opposite of the requirements of Titus 2:4–5. They do not love their husbands, but they love many men, whether simultaneously in adultery or successively by divorce and remarriage. This is the sin *par excellence* against the command of God to be submissive to one's husband. To forsake one's husband and to live with another man is the most extreme form of rebellion and disobedience.

These vile creatures hate the very thought of children and in their hatred for their own children, murder them before they can see the light of day. If a child comes in spite of their precautions, they regard him as a hindrance and a bother, ignore him, and farm him out as quickly as possible to nursery school and babysitters.

According to these women, true happiness is not to be found in the activity of a wife and the activity of a worker at home. This is drudgery and slavery from which they must be liberated. They seek happiness in a career, a job outside the home, or in gadding about.

In contrast to this madness, let the Christian wife have a sound mind, knowing the truth about her calling, not from magazines and novels but from holy scripture. Let her take as examples, not the wretched heroines of television but holy Sarah and the other saintly women. Let her consider what God says about wives, marital faithfulness, children, housewifery, and obedience. God's word on this subject is the truth. It is the highest wisdom. Here, too, the wisdom of the world is mere foolishness, nothing more. God's word calls the Christian woman to a work that is of the greatest worth. The life of the young woman described in the text is not drudgery. On the contrary, her life is glorious and her labor is important.

> Who can find a virtuous woman? for her price is far above rubies. The heart of her husband doth safely trust in her... She will do him good and not evil... She looketh well to the ways of her household, and eateth not the bread of idleness... Many daughters have done virtuously, but thou excellest them all. (Prov. 31:10–31)

Even the angels of heaven are not so glorious, nor their work so important.

The Fear of God

Only a God-fearing young woman can and will fulfill this high calling. This is why Proverbs 31 concludes its description of the virtuous woman by saying, "Favour is deceitful, and beauty is vain: but a woman that feareth the LORD, she shall be praised" (v. 30). Doing the duty of a wife is simply a matter of fearing the Lord. This is true of the calling of the wife to be in subjection to her husband. It is God's authority that is vested in the husband.

Whether or not a wife will call her husband lord, therefore, depends on whether or not she calls God Lord. Her reverence for her husband depends on her reverence for God. The Christian wife is motivated to carry out her calling by her fear of the Lord God. She does not do it for her husband's sake, her children's sake, or her own sake, but for the Lord's sake. She behaves herself as a good wife so that she may thus show her thankfulness to God for his salvation of her and so that he may be praised by her, particularly by her reflection in her married life of the behavior of the church toward Christ. Therefore, although her husband may be unappreciative, often derelict in his own duty, and even an unbeliever, the Christian wife faithfully and joyfully continues in her calling.

An implication of this for the believing young man is that as he looks for a wife, he must make this the all-important question: does she fear God? May he believe, and not have to find out by bitter experience, that favor is deceitful and beauty, vain.

To a God-fearing wife it is important that God's word not be blasphemed, especially that it not be blasphemed on account of her.

This is what the text holds before the Christian wife as her purpose for heeding her calling. She must love her husband, love her children, work at home, and be submissive "so that the word of God be not blasphemed" (Titus 2:5).

There is a close, inseparable connection between the word of God that Christians confess and their conduct in the world. If they walk wickedly, they bring reproach upon the word of God. When they walk uprightly, by the power of the word itself, they bring praise upon the word of God, for in this case they are doing "the things which become sound doctrine" (Titus 2:1). When the world sees a wife who professes Christ Jesus living insolently and evilly against her husband, not only do they mock her and her marriage, but they also speak evil of the word of God that the wife confesses. She gives occasion to the world to hold God's word in contempt, as if it did not possess the power to make any real difference in the life of God's people or as if the word of God tolerated a rebellious wife. If nothing else touches you, let this move you to heed your calling as a wife. The fact that God's word is blasphemed by the bad behavior of a wife implies that God's word is praised by her good behavior. Even the world must glorify God when they see Christian wives living with their husbands in accordance with the text. These are powerful motives for a believing woman. She detests all blasphemy of God and his word. She loves to have God's word praised. Compelled by these incentives, the God-fearing woman will be submissive and sound-minded.

"He Maketh Wars to Cease"

The marriage of the Christian man who dwells with his wife according to knowledge and the Christian woman who submits and is sound-minded is glorious and delightful. In starkest contrast to it stand the marriages of the world. In the world marriage is the battlefield on which a vicious, relentless struggle rages between the tyrant-husband and the rebel-wife. Now the one, now the other is temporarily victorious. At present in our society the rebellious woman has the upper hand. If the world lasts, the male will again assert himself, overthrow the woman's dominance, and rule her more tyrannically than before. The Christian marriage is radically different. The husband rules in love. The wife submits in love. Marriage, thus, is not a framework for bitterest strife and mutual destruction, but a relationship of fellowship, joy, and mutual help. There is peace.

This is possible! This is expected! This is the Christian's calling! It belongs to the great salvation of the sovereign grace of God in Jesus Christ.

Husbands and wives must pray for this without doubting. They are called to work to realize this, to the glory of God's word—and for their own happiness.

5

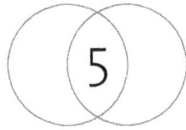

Sex in Marriage

Now concerning the things whereof ye wrote unto me: It is good for a man not to touch a woman. Nevertheless, to avoid fornication, let every man have his own wife, and let every woman have her own husband. Let the husband render unto the wife due benevolence: and likewise also the wife unto the husband. The wife hath not power of her own body, but the husband: and likewise also the husband hath not power of his own body, but the wife. Defraud ye not one the other, except it be with consent for a time, that ye may give yourselves to fasting and prayer; and come together again, that Satan tempt you not for your incontinency. But I speak this by permission, and not of commandment. For I would that all men were even as I myself. But every man hath his proper gift of God, one after this manner, and another after that. I say therefore to the unmarried and widows, It is good for them if they abide even as I. But if they cannot contain, let them marry: for it is better to marry than to burn. —1 Corinthians 7:1–9

There is hesitancy on the part of the church to treat the reality of sex openly and frankly. Insofar as this is a reaction against the shameless openness of the world regarding its perversion of sex, the hesitancy of the church is understandable. Like Sodom of old, the world today glories in its shame. However, modesty with respect to sex is always proper. It is not the expression of a prudish Puritanism, but an aspect of the chastity that God requires in his people. After the fall God gave Adam and Eve clothes to cover their nakedness.

Nevertheless, the reluctance of the church to speak on sex is deplorable, especially for the sake of the youth of the congregation. Unfortunately, the silence of the church is often matched by the silence of the parents. The church and home only refer to sex negatively, in condemning its abuse. They say little or nothing positive about sex—about the sexual nature of people and the rightful place that sex has in the life of a man and his wife. This is a mistake, as it is always a mistake to concentrate on condemning the abuse of a thing instead of explaining its proper use.

The timidity of the church and the Christian home is all the more unwise today in view of the boldness of the world. The world is not silent about sex. It proclaims sex openly, loudly, and constantly—to the point of nausea. Everything is pressed into the service of peddling a vile and wicked view of sex. Sexual immorality is the message of books, songs, and magazines; of radio, television, and movies; of dress; of advertising; indeed, of every phase of our culture. This inescapable barrage not only gives false instruction about sex, but it also aims at tempting God's people, especially God's young people. It deceives men, for it teaches the lie about sex. It also plays on a powerful aspect of man's nature, stirs it up, and drives it toward a base and evil expression. It is not good that the church, in the face of this assault, remains silent.

In addition, the hesitancy and silence of the church and Christian home are wrong because often they are due to fear. This fear stems from the notion that sex is inherently shameful and evil. This error has serious consequences. Not only does it leave a false impression on the youth, but it also has troublesome effects on the marriages in the church and on the personal peace of married saints. Paul exposes the falsity of this notion in 1 Corinthians 7:1–9, where he sets forth in detail the truth concerning sex in marriage.

Frank Treatment

As is evident in this passage, scripture treats the reality and use of sex with an openness and frankness that contrast sharply with our hesitancy and embarrassment. This becomes very plain, for example, in a passage like Proverbs 5. This chapter is instruction of a son by a believing father. It provides a pattern for all of us fathers to follow in instructing our children. There is pointed, plain, down-to-earth warning against fornication, including a detailed description of the bitter consequences of fornication. "For the lips of a strange woman drop as an honeycomb, and her mouth is smoother than oil: But her end is bitter as wormwood, sharp as a two-edged sword. Her feet go down to death; her steps take hold on hell" (Prov. 5:3–5). But there is also plain, positive instruction concerning the propriety and joy of the sexual relationship in marriage with one's own wife. "Let thy fountain be blessed: and rejoice with the wife of thy youth. Let her be as the loving hind and pleasant roe; let her breasts satisfy thee at all times; and be thou ravished always with her love" (vv. 18–19). This same openness occurs throughout the Song of Solomon. This is holy scripture, God's word to the church—men, women, and children—given for preaching, reading, and study. It is not off limits. It is instruction that is necessary for God's people as they work out their salvation in the world.

The first nine verses of 1 Corinthians 7 also are instruction to the whole church on the subject of sex in marriage. The church at Corinth wrote Paul, asking questions about sex and marriage. That is why he introduces Chapter 7 by saying, "Now concerning the things whereof ye wrote unto me" (v. 1). In an open letter he answers their questions, giving them—and us—this necessary, practical instruction.

What is at once striking is the apparently different view of marriage that the apostle has here in comparison with his view of marriage in Ephesians 5, where Paul has the loftiest, most ideal view of marriage. He sees marriage as the mystery of Christ and the church. In 1 Corinthians 7 the same apostle looks at marriage differently. He takes what seems to be, in contrast to Ephesians 5, a low, practical view of marriage. The reason for marrying is "to avoid fornication" (1 Cor. 7:2), that is, so that the man or woman does not give in to the sexual desire by committing fornication. A man is to marry if he cannot "contain"; that is, if he cannot control the sexual aspect of his nature. Paul writes, "It is better to marry than to burn" (v. 9).

This difference in viewpoint is a problem to some people. There seems to be irreconcilable difference between the lofty, heavenly view on marriage of Ephesians 5 and the "low, earthy" outlook of 1 Corinthians 7. For this reason some ignore or minimize the truth concerning marriage found in 1 Corinthians 7 and concentrate on the teaching of Ephesians 5.

In fact, however, there is no disagreement between Ephesians 5 and 1 Corinthians 7, between marriage as the mystery of Christ and the church and "to avoid fornication let every man have his own wife" (1 Cor. 7:2). These chapters give two distinct aspects of the reality of marriage, and these two aspects taken together make up the whole truth about marriage. Ephesians 5 gives the lofty principle of marriage: it is the symbol of Christ's union with the church. 1 Corinthians 7 concerns itself with the practical application of this glorious principle in the lives of the saints. The word of God always includes principle and practice, doctrine and life. The principle, be it ever so lofty and glorious, does not rule out practice, but it *rules* our practice. Within our view of marriage as the symbol of Christ's relation to the church, there is room for the practical consideration of marriage as the God-ordained means by which the sexual nature of the man and the woman find fulfillment. The reason this down-to-earth view of marriage does not conflict with the lofty idea of Ephesians 5 is that sex is not inherently shameful and evil but is a good creature of God.

The Goodness of Sex

In contrast to the thinking of the world, we have a high view of sex. It is not inherently animalistic, base, shameful, and evil. It is not a subject fit to be referred to only by innuendoes and to be discussed only in whispers, with smirks and leers. It is not even a human weakness or fleshly blemish that has to be catered to, unfortunately, in marriage, as if in marriage we make the best of a bad thing. Paul's teaching in 1 Corinthians 7 is not that the sexual nature of man is bad. He does say that it is good for a man not to touch a woman, that is, not to have sexual relations with a woman in marriage (v. 1). He desires that all men be as he is, that is, unmarried (v. 7). He tells the unmarried and the widows that it is good for them if they remain single (v. 8). It is not absolutely required of God's people to marry. It is not shameful to be unmarried. Being single is good, an excellent thing. Indeed, from a certain viewpoint and under certain circumstances, it is better to be single than to be married.

But this does not imply that sexual activity in marriage is really an evil and that this is the reason it is better to be single.

For the apostle recommends remaining single only to those who have the special gift from God that enables them to "contain" (vv. 7, 9). And then, there is nothing good in being single in itself, as if it were intrinsically superior to being married, but being single allows one to devote himself more fully to the Lord and to his kingdom (vv. 32, 34). This, however, is the exception, not the rule. The rule is that every man have his own wife and that every woman have her own husband (v. 2). In marriage the sexual relationship is good.

The inherent goodness of sex within the bond of marriage is due to its having been created in the man and his wife by God in the beginning. It is not the case that the man became sexual, fleshly, after the fall. Sex is not the result of sin. According to Genesis 1:28, God blessed Adam and Eve with sexuality before the fall: "And God blessed them, and God said unto them, Be fruitful, and multiply, and replenish the earth." Sexuality was a blessing. God spoke a word of blessing on the sixth day that gave Adam and Eve a sexual nature. It was no small part of the bliss of paradise that Adam and Eve lived together as man and wife, including the sexual union. They would have had children in the state of perfection had they not so quickly sinned. No shame was attached to this, as Genesis 2:25 shows: "And they were both naked, the man and his wife, and were not ashamed." Also this aspect of creation was judged good by God at the conclusion of his creative work: "And God saw every thing that he had made, and, behold, it was very good. And the evening and the morning were the sixth day" (Gen. 1:31).

What God has called clean, let not man call unclean. To prohibit marriage because sex is allegedly base and evil is the doctrine of devils (1 Tim. 4:1, 3). Marriage in its entirety is a good creature of God, made for us and given to us to be enjoyed with thanksgiving. Our criticism of the world is not that it esteems sex highly, but that it abases sex, refusing to honor it as a good creation of God.

Sex was corrupted through man's fall into sin. Fallen, sinful man pollutes this aspect of his nature as well as every other. But fallen mankind's perversion of sex is special; mankind concentrates on abusing this aspect of life. This is because sex itself is something special by virtue of God's creation. It belongs to marriage, and marriage is the earthly sign of the communion of God and his people, a symbol of the covenant. Therefore, the devil works especially hard to obtain the special perversion of sex among men. But the grace of our Lord Jesus Christ restores the right attitude toward sex and the right use of sex in the elect believer. The goodness of the sexual relationship concerning believers underlies all of 1 Corinthians 7.

But sex is a good thing only in marriage. Outside of marriage, sexual relationships are sinful. This is clearly Paul's teaching when he writes, "To avoid fornication, let every man have his own wife" (v. 2). Fornication is sexual activity by the unmarried. It is sin; therefore, the saint must avoid it. The way to avoid it is by marrying. The sexual relationship of a married person with someone other than one's own mate is also sinful. This is implied by Paul in 1 Corinthians 7:5, where he tells married people to live together sexually "that Satan tempt you not for your incontinency." Extramarital relationships are temptations of the devil, sins, and the means by which he tries to devour men.

Sex and the Singles

Everywhere scripture condemns sex outside of marriage as sin and holds up sex in marriage as approved. 1 Thessalonians 4:3–4 says that it is God's will that we abstain from fornication.

The proper behavior is that each of us "possess his vessel in sanctification and honour" (v. 4), that is, be married. Hebrews 13:4 declares that "whoremongers and adulterers God will judge." However, "marriage is honourable in all, and the bed undefiled." This truth of God concerning sex has a practical purpose. It sheds light on the path of the married and unmarried saints, so that they walk wisely and uprightly. The unmarried saint may not commit fornication.

Bitterest evils result from fornication, evils that not only destroy the body but also scar the soul. This is so because fornication is an evil, a sin against God. The young saint's avoidance of the abuse of sex in fornication should take into account the right use of sex in marriage. That is, the young woman keeps in mind that her beauty is for the young man who will be her husband, and the young man remembers that his strength is for the young woman who will be his wife. Consciously, the young man refuses to become one body with harlots, because he is to become one flesh with his wife (1 Cor. 6:16). The way to escape the pitfall of fornication is to avoid all that stirs up lust. This is what Paul means when he cries out, "Flee fornication" (1 Cor. 6:18). Run away from it. Shun pornographic books and magazines; do not attend the movie or watch the television program that promotes sexual immorality; do not wear clothing that entices men to lust; do not play with sexual fire in dating.

Instead, marry! This is also part of the practical wisdom of God to the unmarried. Marriage is the safeguard against the evil of fornication and the solution to the problem of our sexual nature. This is Paul's teaching in 1 Corinthians 7:9: "But if they cannot contain, let them marry: for it is better to marry than to burn."

We must be careful that we do not make burning the sole consideration in marrying. We must also marry "in the Lord," according to verse 39. The young believer must choose a believing mate. So important and binding is this injunction that if a believing mate cannot be found, there must be no marriage, even though one burns. God will then give grace so that the believer is able to contain. Nor is the sexual desire the foundation of marriage. Never build a marriage on it as if sex were the only thing, or even the main thing in the marriage. This is precisely the foolish, costly mistake of the world, particularly in today's society. Those marriages are as flimsy as the foundation on which they are built.

Today sex is virtually a god. The church must condemn this idolatry and resist it. The basic thing in the Christian's life is his personal marriage to God by a true and living faith. If God should prevent marriage for one of his children, as he sometimes does, the reality of marriage is still his because he enjoys the covenant friendship of God in Christ. If God makes one a eunuch for the kingdom's sake, he is not hopelessly deprived or impoverished, but still rich, for he has God. Not sex, not earthly marriage, not any creature, but God is God.

The foundation of marriage must be the couple's spiritual oneness: their unity in Christ Jesus and their unity in the truth of scripture. Not their sexual compatibility, but their spiritual compatibility is basic. This limits the young believer to believing members of the church, but it also warns a young person against rushing into marriage with the first available young woman or young man simply because you burn, even though both of you are believers. There must be the conviction, through prayer, that this person is knit to you in a special way and is God's answer to your prayer for a husband or a wife. As a means to this end, dating has a legitimate place.

None of this, however, takes away from the fact that marriage is the remedy for burning. It does not only serve to prevent fornication, but it is as well the remedy for the internal burning of the sexual desire.

Sex and the Married

So far, we have considered sex and the unmarried saints. What light does God's word shed on the life of the married in this regard? Paul teaches in this passage that it is obligatory for both the husband and the wife to live sexually with the other. This is what he admonishes in 1 Corinthians 7:3: "Let the husband render unto the wife due benevolence: and likewise also the wife unto the husband." The words that the translators of the King James Version render as "due benevolence" refer to married persons giving their bodies to each other in the sexual union and describe this as a debt that each owes to the other. That this is so is made clear by verse 4, where Paul gives the ground for what he commanded in verse 3: "The wife hath not power of her own body, but the husband: and likewise also the husband hath not power of his own body, but the wife." Here "power" means authority.

To give himself to his wife is a debt that the husband owes the wife, just as it is a debt that the wife owes to her husband, to give herself to him. It is a debt, because the husband has authority over the body of the wife, and the wife over the body of the husband. Their bodies are no longer only their own, but also the others. This is due to the intimacy of marriage, the amazing closeness of the man and his wife: married persons have become one flesh! Therefore, for husbands and wives to withhold themselves from each other is robbery. "Defraud, ye not one the other," writes Paul in verse 5.

But let us be sure to see the Christian, the Christ-like uniqueness of the apostle's viewpoint here, a viewpoint we must incorporate into our marriages. In the thinking of the natural man, the marriage partner is only a means for one's self-gratification.

Our main concern by nature is, how can and should my mate please me? Then the sexual relationship is a matter of our taking from our husbands or wives and of our using each other. The apostle requires us to view the sexual relationship from a radically different perspective. He points out that the main concern of the husband should not be, "How shall my wife please me?" but "How shall I please my wife?" For the husband, it is not the question, "What does my wife owe me?" but "What is my debt to my wife?" The same holds for the wife. Paul calls us, in our Christian marriages, to give to the other, to be concerned with the welfare of the other, and to pay our debt to the other. Thus the sexual aspect of marriage is part of genuine love, an expression of that love that does not grasp for self but gives to the other.

Sex is an integral part of married life, and it is an altogether honorable part. It is true, as is the case with all authority, that the authority, or power, that the husband has over the wife's body, and that the wife has over the husband's, must be exercised responsibly. This is done when the authority is directed by our spiritual love for our mates and by our concern for their welfare. But there need not be, and should not be, any injection of gloomy fears and inhibitions into this aspect of marriage. The sexual relationship may and should be free from shame.

A sense of shame with regard to sex has needlessly troubled marriages in the church. The church herself has contributed to such problems, not only by her embarrassed silence on the entire subject of sex but also by giving currency to the notion that sex is inherently shameful through her teaching that sex is good and legitimate only because children result. The implication is that sex itself is evil, but is redeemed by children. In contrast to all such gloomy thinking, the scriptures allow for a joyful freedom in marriage.

For the scriptures regard the sexual aspect of marriage as inherently good, not evil; honorable, not shameful. It is included in the redemption of Christ's cross. Its goodness is apparent in verse 5 of 1 Corinthians 7, where it is brought into the closest proximity to prayer without any hint of incongruity: "That ye may give yourselves to fasting and prayer; and come together again." Therefore, the Christian husband and wife are able to discuss this aspect of their marriage and to do so without embarrassment. Communication between husband and wife on their sexual relationship is implied in the statement of verse 5 that they abstain for a time by mutual consent.

Sex and the Real Marriage

Sex is an honorable aspect of marriage, not only because God created it in the beginning, but also because it serves a purpose in reflecting the marriage of Christ and the church. It points in a unique way to the intimacy of the union of Christ and the church. In the sexual relationship there is a unique realization and expression of the closeness of marriage. The two are one flesh. There is oneness, not only of the bodies but also of the souls. For this reason modesty is proper. It is out of place to make this aspect of our marriage the topic of public conversation. Certainly it is inappropriate, a kind of profanity, to make it the butt of jokes. In our intimate life with Christ, we have secrets that we do not disclose to others and that we would never expose to banter and ridicule. To do so would be to jeopardize that intimate life we have with him. So it is in our earthly marriage.

The sexual relationship also symbolizes the kind of love that Christ has for the church and that the church has for Christ. The love of Christ for us is awesome. It is quite different from the sentimental, ineffectual, easily resisted love of Arminian theology.

Christ's love, and God's love in him, is a relentless, unswerving, demanding, possessive, jealous love, the sovereign love of Reformed theology. It is a love that elects, redeems, regenerates, sanctifies, preserves, and glorifies—all in order that Christ, the bridegroom, may take to himself the church, his bride, as his everlasting possession. In his love Christ wills to have the church for his own, even at the cost of eternal hell. And the love of the beloved church for Christ, in response, is such that the church desires him and gives herself wholly to him. This is the love celebrated ecstatically in the Song of Solomon: "Set me as a seal upon thine heart, as a seal upon thine arm: for love is strong as death; jealousy is cruel as the grave: the coals thereof are coals of fire, which hath a most vehement flame. Many waters cannot quench love, neither can the floods drown it: if a man would give all the substance of his house for love, it would utterly be contemned" (8:6–7).

Basic to this fiery love is that there be two, only two. Christ loves the one church, and the church loves the one Christ only. Any intrusion by another party would ruin the love. This is equally true in earthly marriage. Therefore, Paul does not say, "Let every man have a woman," but he says, "Let every man have his own wife," and "let every woman have her own husband" (1 Cor. 7:2).

Teaching Children about Sex

If this is the truth about sex, only believing parents are able to teach their children about it. The world is unable to do this. They only corrupt our children, whether by their filthy talk; their perverted movies, television programs, and books; or their formal classes of sex education in the public schools. "The natural man receiveth not the things of the Spirit of God: for they are foolishness unto him: neither can he know them, because they are spiritually discerned" (1 Cor. 2:14). But Christians know the truth and are able to educate their children. And this is their duty.

6

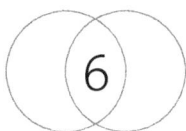

Children
in Marriage

And God blessed them, and God said unto them, Be fruitful, and multiply, and replenish the earth, and subdue it: and have dominion over the fish of the sea, and over the fowl of the air, and over every living thing that moveth upon the earth. —Genesis 1:28

Unto the woman he said, I will greatly multiply thy sorrow and thy conception; in sorrow thou shall bring forth children; and thy desire shall be to thy husband, and he shall rule over thee. —Genesis 3:16

Notwithstanding she shall be saved in childbearing, if they continue in faith and charity and holiness with sobriety. —1 Timothy 2:15

At the present time there is a furor in the world and in the churches over birth control. The Roman Catholic Church is in an uproar over this issue. It has been the teaching of Rome in the past that the practice of birth control by artificial or mechanical means is grave sin. Pope after pope has plainly and emphatically taught this in official documents, or encyclicals. For this reason it is surprising that there is as much amazement at the present pope's teaching, and opposition to it, as there is. This is no new teaching in any respect. Besides, contradiction of the teachings of former popes would jeopardize Rome's doctrine of papal infallibility.

In the past few years, at the insistence of many Roman Catholics, the question of birth control was restudied. Recently, the pope issued an encyclical called *Humanae Vitae* (On the regulation of birth) in which he fully supported Rome's historic teaching regarding birth control and condemned as grave sin every act of birth prevention. Since then a storm of protest has raged in the Roman Church, threatening to some extent even the supremacy of the pope. The world has involved itself in Rome's struggle. Editorialists, educators, social agencies, and even government officials criticize Rome's position. Many were angered by the pope's decision because a project is under way at the present time to limit births on a worldwide scale. The pope's decision, it is feared, will hinder these efforts. Inevitably, the Protestant leaders had something to say. They condemned the Roman doctrine almost unanimously. Most of Protestantism advocates birth control as godly behavior and condemns the failure to practice it as immoral.

This entire question and the controversy that surrounds it affects believers. The issue is out in the open. The practice itself of birth control becomes a problem for believing husbands and wives. The question is raised, what must the attitude of the Christian husband and wife be toward birth control?

Not only are the standards by which believers judge the issue, and the conclusions to which they come, different from the standards and conclusions of the world, but the very point of view with which believers consider the issue is different. The underlying issue, and fundamental question, is, what is the place of children in marriage? Bearing and rearing children is an aspect of the reality of marriage. Since marriage from beginning to end is a divine institution, not our thinking but God's will is determinative for our behavior in marriage, also regarding having or not having children. Therefore, we look to God's word, the holy scriptures, for the answer to this basic question: what is the place of children in the marriage of believers?

Childless Marriage

Erroneous explanations of the place of children in marriage have been found in the church. These are explanations that err by overemphasizing the importance of children in marriage. Perhaps the exaggeration is due to men's feeling that they have to fight very vehemently against the prevalent disparagement of children. Whatever the motive, such exaggerations are harmful. They thoughtlessly injure some of God's people—for example, the childless couple—and they do damage to the truth of marriage. These exaggerations ascribe one purpose to marriage, namely, having children, and virtually deny the completeness and worth of marriage apart from children.

Those who preach such notions probably suppose that they are stressing the importance of children. In fact, they are denying the significance of marriage. A marriage between a man and a woman is complete in itself. For marriage in its deepest significance is the symbol of the relationship of love and fellowship between Christ and the church. When a believing man and his believing wife live together in love, according to the pattern of Christ and his bride, God's highest purpose with marriage is realized, even though there are no children in the marriage. Although God may withhold children from a married couple, the husband and the wife have during all their life important and demanding work to do. They have the lofty calling of showing forth the mystery of Christ and the church. They have the high calling of fulfilling the mutual responsibilities of husband and wife in their life together.

Sex and Procreation

Closely related to the error of making marriage depend on children is the assertion that the only legitimate use of sex is the begetting of children. Undoubtedly, the reason for such a statement is fear of the trend today to sunder sex and procreation. But scripture makes clear that the sexual relationship between a man and his wife has a purpose and value other than that of begetting children. It is an aspect of the amazing and joyful intimacy of marriage and an expression of the unique relationship of love in marriage. It is an important part of fellowship in marriage.

With this use of the sexual relationship, however, God has mingled another use, namely, the begetting of children. The two purposes of God with regard to sex in marriage have been joined together very closely. In the practice of birth control, man separates, or tries to separate, what God has joined together. Man tries to retain the expression and enjoyment of the intimacy of marriage while excluding the bringing forth of children. At once the question arises, does man have the right to do this? May he so separate the two uses of the sexual relationship? In addition the question arises whether man can really do this. Of course, we know that man today, with his pills and devices, can effectively prevent the conception of a child. But does he retain the intimacy, the fellowship? There is some fear today that certain means of birth control are dangerous because they adversely affect the mysterious make-up and workings of the body. There is at least as much reason to fear that man's tampering with sex, in the interest of frustrating one of the functions God has given it—namely, the begetting of children—adversely affects the mysterious make-up and workings of the souls of a man and his wife and thus hinders the intimacy of the marital relationship, as well as the procreative aspect.

For us God's word is decisive. Between us and the world there is a radical difference regarding our view of marriage. It is not the case that basically we both have the same view of marriage but that we differ only on certain details of married life. Rather, we have fundamentally different views of marriage. The difference is between a God-centered view of marriage and a man-centered view. For unbelievers, marriage begins and ends with themselves: their happiness, their pleasure, their comfort, and their will. Our marriages, however, begin and end with God. Our marriages are not ultimately for our sakes, but for God's sake; they are not for our ease and pleasure, but they are in the service of God's purpose and for his honor. Our marriages are his in the fullest sense. Right behavior in marriage, therefore, consists of submitting to God's will as he makes it known in his word. We may not answer the hard questions of married life by considering how we think or feel at the moment, but we must look to God's word for his will. Then, even though painfully at times, we must again and again bring our wills into conformity with his.

Children in Three Stages of History

God's word speaks of childbearing and the place of children in marriage at three distinct stages of human history. These three stages are represented in the three texts quoted at the beginning of this chapter: Genesis 1:28, Genesis 3:16, and 1 Timothy 2:15. These texts teach us the place of children in marriage according to God's original institution in paradise before the fall; the effect of the fall on childbearing; and the significance of childbearing for believing women in the church today.

Genesis 1:28 is the powerful word of God to the just-created man and his wife that bestows on them the gift of sex and which commands them to bring forth children by it. "And God blessed them, and God said unto them, Be fruitful, and multiply, and replenish the earth, and subdue it: and have dominion over the fish of the sea, and over the fowl of the air, and over every living thing that moveth upon the earth." As given originally, the sexual relation in marriage has as a divine purpose of fruitfulness and multiplying, that is, the bringing forth of children. This was God's will with it from the beginning, and God made this purpose of begetting children something inherent in sex itself. The goal of Adam and Eve's bringing forth children was man's exercising dominion over all the earth. Adam and Eve alone could not do this; full dominion over the earthly creation demanded a race of godly kings and queens.

Genesis 3:16 instructs that the fall into sin affected motherhood and childbearing: "Unto the woman he said, I will greatly multiply thy sorrow and thy conception; in sorrow thou shalt bring forth children; and thy desire shall be to thy husband, and he shall rule over thee." This text speaks of the chastisement God inflicted on the woman because of her part in the fall. The idea is that there will be hardships that God brings into the life of all women generally. From now on, enduring these hardships will be part of the life of the woman. The chastisement was an increase of the woman's conception of children and an increase of the woman's sorrow in this conception. In other words, the woman will conceive children more frequently than she would have before the fall. Also, she will bring forth these children in sorrow. This sorrow of childbearing does not refer only to the physical pain at the time of delivery, although this by itself would be severe, but it also refers to the physical pain that often accompanies carrying the child before birth and to the physical hardships a mother endures as she rears her children.

However, the sorrow of childbearing does not refer exclusively to physical pain and hardship. The bitterest sorrow of all is the sorrow of bearing and rearing sinful children. Think of the grief of mother Eve as she watched her firstborn son grow up a godless, unbelieving man, and think of her sorrow as she buried a son whose life was cut off in youth by the hand of his own brother, her son.

The scriptures also speak of the motherhood of regenerated women. This sheds light on another distinct aspect of the truth of children in marriage. In 1 Timothy 2:15, after Paul has noted that it was the woman who was deceived and who first sinned in paradise, he says, "Notwithstanding she shall be saved in childbearing, if they continue in faith and charity and holiness with sobriety." Such is the importance of childbearing that, as a rule, it is the way in which God saves believing women.

Children a Blessing

It is clear from all these passages of scripture that begetting and bearing children is the will of God. He made it an integral part of marriage in the beginning. He imposed the painful aspects of childbearing on the woman after the fall. He sanctifies childbearing in the church, so that it is a way of salvation for believing women.

But what must be seen in these passages, above all, is that childbearing is a blessing to believers. In the beginning God blessed Adam and Eve with fruitfulness: "And God blessed them, and God said...Be fruitful" (Gen. 1:28). Fruitfulness in marriage was a good thing, nor did childbearing, as such, become a curse after the fall. Although we read that God cursed the serpent and that God cursed the ground for man's sake, we do not read that

God cursed Eve when he imposed on her the hardships of motherhood. The sorrows attending conception were chastisements for her, not a curse. Besides, it was not childbearing itself that was inflicted on the woman after the fall but an increase of childbearing and an increase of sorrow. That childbearing is a blessing of God in Christ to believing women is strongly emphasized by 1 Timothy 2:15. It is now a way of salvation for them. This, then, is the way believers view children in their marriages: children are a blessing.

The view of the world is radically different. Underlying all of the world's arguments in favor of birth prevention is the conviction that childbearing and children are a curse. This is the heart of the issue regarding birth control: are children a blessing or a curse? The world has certain grounds for its contention that children are a curse, but these grounds are flimsy and certainly do not weigh with God's people. The world screams for birth control because of a population explosion that may cause famine. Even if this were so, the danger of a famine is not in North America, where it is played up, but in countries like India. In the United States parents are more capable of supporting large families financially than people ever have been before. Our land is capable of supplying an abundance of luxuries, much more than the bare needs of its people. A country that spends scores of billions of dollars to go to the moon, that spends billions of dollars for a war in Vietnam, that has much of its farm land in the soil bank, and that wastes its resources prodigally is not even worthy of a hearing when it tells us to limit our families because of a shortage of natural resources. The world also makes a feeble attempt to support its program of birth prevention by suggesting that fewer children are better reared. But the falsity of this claim is proved by our society. In our society among those whose citizenship is in this world, it seems to be a rule that the fewer the children, the less attention is paid to them and the worse their rearing is.

These are the world's arguments, based on the world's thinking and geared to the world's goals. All of them are man-centered. They appeal to man's desire for luxuries—luxuries that a large family might have to forgo. They appeal to the woman's desire to have much time for herself, which is impossible if she has many children. Let us confess that they find a ready response in our flesh also: children, especially many children, are a bother and a nuisance, because they interfere with our fun and games.

God is not in all the world's thoughts on the matter of family planning. They know no sovereign Lord of heaven and earth, who regulates births according to an all-wise counsel. They have no heavenly Father upon whom to depend for daily bread. We must not be influenced by the world's arguments, nor may we adopt its viewpoint. There may be too many worldlings on earth, but are there too many children of God? God's purpose with children in the beginning was that there be a race of godly kings who subject the creation to him. Today, because of his covenant of grace in Jesus Christ, God realizes this purpose in the children of believers. This is the way we should look at the number of people on earth.

We should also fortify ourselves against the state's illegitimate intrusion into this aspect of our lives. The state has no authority to dictate the size of our families. At present the state subjects us to moral pressure in order to make us limit our families to 2.3 children. But already the state begins to make threatening noises about penalizing those who have more children than it permits. The time may very well come when the state demands obedience to its law regulating the size of families. As Christians we are bound to provide for our families, to rear them well, and to train our children to work, but we are not bound to obey any law that decrees the number of children we may have. Over against the state's will that we not bear children stands the will of God expressed by Paul in 1 Timothy 5:14: "I will therefore that the younger women marry, bear children, guide the house, give none occasion to the adversary to speak reproachfully."

The Sorrow of Motherhood

There is one hard aspect of childbearing that does weigh heavily with the church. This is the sorrow of motherhood. There is the physical toil and pain of giving birth and of rearing the children. There is also the labor and sorrow of the mother's soul as she carries out this calling. The sorrow of motherhood is great! God greatly multiplied the woman's sorrow and conception so that the sorrow in which she brings forth children is a great sorrow (Gen. 3:16). In a certain sense the mother must give her life away for the sake of the children. This is the burden of the woman because of sin. Nor does God bless the motherhood of a believing woman by removing all the hardships and making motherhood easy in her case. God does bless her as a mother, but not in this way. The burden of sorrow and the burden of the increase of pregnancy remain also for her.

But what now is the solution for the believing woman? Where does her salvation lie? Is the answer this, that she evades the burden by refusing to have children? Or is the answer this, that she finds grace and strength in Jesus Christ to bear the burden of motherhood? The unbelieving women of the world simply evade the burden by preventing the birth of children. They reject motherhood with its great sorrow. They seek fulfillment outside the home in other vocations. Generally speaking, however, there has never been a more troubled, dissatisfied, unhappy, and ungodly woman than the modern emancipated American woman. This psychological and spiritual wretchedness bears out what Paul wrote: "She shall be saved in [through] childbearing" (1 Tim. 2:15).

Motherhood is hard. But the answer for women who profess godliness is not to escape it, as is possible today, for she is saved by childbearing. The apostle certainly means the spiritual salvation of Christ crucified and risen. Ordinarily the eternal salvation of the believing woman is tied up with childbearing. It is not the case that the woman enjoys salvation for the first time when she bears a child. Neither is it so that childbearing itself saves in any sense. The text shows this when it adds, "If they continue in faith and charity and holiness with sobriety." Rather, childbearing is ordinarily the way, the earthly way of life, in which God saves believing women in the sense of maintaining their salvation and enriching it.

The believing woman, therefore, faced with the sorrows of motherhood, must respond, not by avoiding this difficult way but by seeking the grace of Christ to endure the sorrows and to perform the labor. And the church, sympathetic toward the sorrows of the mothers in Israel, does not begin to preach the worldly wisdom of family planning, but she strengthens and comforts with the word of God. She directs mothers to the strong and compassionate savior, Jesus Christ, whose grace is sufficient for all their burdens. He knows the great sorrows of motherhood. He himself grew up in a family of at least seven children and possibly more. Matthew 13:55–56 informs us that Jesus had four brothers and at least two sisters. He knows by experience the needs of mothers with large families, having seen these needs in his own beloved mother. He is able to give grace to help in time of need.

The Joy of Motherhood

Christ strengthens and gladdens parents in the church by proclaiming in his word that he saves their children. God's covenant with his people, as well today as in Old Testament times, includes as a precious element that God will be the God of their children after them. On the very day of the dawning of the new dispensation, when God's church had come to maturity, the Holy Spirit had Peter cry out, "For the promise is unto you, and to your children" (Acts 2:39). Thus throughout the New Testament the children of believers are included in the church as members (Eph. 6:1–4; Col. 3:20–21).

Christ builds up his church from the children of believers. He makes these children kings who not only will rule with him everlastingly, but who also begin to rule the creation as servants of God already now, so that God's purpose with children in Genesis 1:28 is realized in them. "Out of the mouth of babes and sucklings thou hast perfected praise" (Matt. 21:16). This is why our children are a blessing, not a curse. This is the joy of the godly mother that swallows up all her sorrows, especially the sorrow of bearing sinful children. This makes all of the toil and sacrifice of believing parents worthwhile. They rear children who are "an heritage of the LORD" (Ps. 127:3) so that these children may praise God in time and eternity.

Already in Eve's case the joy of motherhood had precedence over the sorrows. God promised her the seed that would bruise the devil's head: Jesus Christ and the elect multitude from Eve who are in Christ. Then, and only then, God spoke of the great sorrows of childbearing.

In light of this, it is not surprising that in history the devil has been the outstanding advocate in the church of birth prevention and, failing in that, of the murder of the infants of believers. It was he who moved the Pharaoh of Exodus 1 to enslave and afflict Israel so that they would not multiply. When God frustrated this plan and blessed Israel with many children, the devil attempted to murder the newly born male children. He knows that many children are a strength of the church because of the covenant of God.

God's Large Family

Even the fruitfulness of the marriage of believers belongs to the symbolism of marriage as a picture of the marriage of Christ and the church. Marriage is the mystery of Christ and the church. Christ begets many sons and daughters by his word and Spirit.

He has a large family, a multitude no man can number. To them he is willing to devote his care. Christ even gave his life for them. Christ brings these children forth from, and rears them by, the church, his bride. The union of Christ and the church is fruitful in many children of God. The church is the mother of the saints by the power of the grace of Christ. So we sing in a version of Psalm 87:

When the Lord shall count the nations,
Sons and daughters He shall see,
Born to endless life in Zion,
And their joyful song shall be,
"Blessed Zion, All our fountains are in thee,
Blessed Zion, All our fountains are in thee."[1]

So closely connected are the symbol, our marriages, and the reality, Christ's union with the church, that God uses the symbol to bring forth those who participate in the reality.

Therefore, Christian husbands and wives are still addressed

---

1 No. 237:3, in *The Psalter with Doctrinal Standards, Liturgy, Church Order, and Added Chorale Section*, reprinted and revised edition of the 1912 United Presbyterian *Psalter* (Grand Rapids, MI: Wm. B. Eerdmans Publishing Co., 1927; rev. ed. 1995).

by the Lord in the words of the prophet in Jeremiah 29:5–6: "Build ye houses, and dwell in them; and plant gardens, and eat the fruit of them; Take ye wives, and beget sons and daughters; and take wives for your sons, and give your daughters to husbands, that they may bear sons and daughters; that ye may be increased there, and not diminished."

7

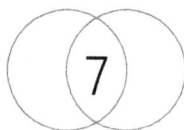

The Forbidding
of Divorce

*It hath been said, Whosoever shall put away his wife, let him give
her a writing of divorcement: But I say unto you, That whosoever shall put away his wife, saving for the cause of fornication,
causeth her to commit adultery: and whosoever shall marry her
that is divorced committeth adultery.* —Matthew 5:31–32

As we continue to examine God's word on marriage, we
come to the subject of divorce. Churches that care very little
about the truth of marriage are concerned about divorce. Even
the unbelieving world is alarmed at the high rate of divorce. The
explanation of this concern and alarm is not that horror takes
hold on them because of the wicked that forsake God's law, as
Psalm 119:53 puts it, but that divorce disrupts their lives and
causes severe problems in human society.

Some of God's children have a special interest in the biblical teaching concerning divorce because they are divorced, or
because their marriages are plagued with serious problems. But
the truth about divorce is of great importance to all members

of the church, the unmarried as well as the married. All of us are responsible for the purity of the church and for the spiritual strength and welfare of the church that lives on after us. It is here, on the issue of divorce, that the obedience of the church to the truth of marriage is put to the test. By her stand on divorce, the church either maintains or fatally compromises the truth of marriage, both for herself and for future generations.

We must be careful not to consider divorce in abstraction from marriage. Divorce can be viewed rightly only in the light of all that has previously been said concerning marriage. Divorce is a negative. The positive that it negates is marriage. Divorce is the separation of two who have been made one in marriage. Therefore, in order to judge divorce correctly, we need to remember the truth about marriage: who instituted marriage; of what marriage is a symbol; what actually takes place when a man and woman marry; and what the laws of God are that govern marriage.

Christ showed that divorce must be viewed and judged in the light of the truth of marriage in Matthew 19. When the Pharisees asked him about divorce (v. 3), he replied by first stating the truth of marriage in verses 4–6. The essence of marriage is "they are no more twain, but one flesh." Then, in light of the truth of marriage and in complete dependence on it, Christ expressed the law concerning divorce: "what therefore God hath joined together, let not man put asunder" (v. 6).

Although the title of this chapter is negative, "The Forbidding of Divorce," the main idea and purpose will be positive. The topic has been put in the negative form deliberately. The negative form serves to make the truth sharp and clear. As never before the church today must hear and know this truth: no divorce! The negative title is also faithful to the teaching of Jesus in Matthew 5:31–32, for this text is a condemnation of divorce. Nevertheless, the text condemns divorce in the interest of the sanctity, the intimacy, and the beauty of the bond of marriage.

Deuteronomy 24 on Divorce

In Matthew 5 Jesus is obviously contrasting his teaching on divorce with another teaching. That other teaching is Moses' regulation regarding divorce for Israel in the Old Testament. When Jesus declares in verse 31, "It hath been said, Whosoever shall put away his wife, let him give her a writing of divorcement," he refers to the regulation concerning divorce in Deuteronomy 24:1–4:

1. When a man hath taken a wife, and married her, and it come to pass that she find no favour in his eyes, because he hath found some uncleanness in her: then let him write her a bill of divorcement, and give it in her hand, and send her out of his house.

2. And when she is departed out of his house, she may go and be another man's wife.

3. And if the latter husband hate her, and write her a bill of divorcement, and giveth it in her hand, and sendeth her out of his house; or if the latter husband die, which took her to be his wife;

4. Her former husband, which sent her away, may not take her again to be his wife, after that she is defiled; for that is abomination before the LORD: and thou shalt not cause the land to sin, which the LORD thy God giveth thee for an inheritance.

This Old Testament regulation is so important in Matthew 19. The Pharisees tempted Jesus concerning divorce by asking him,

"Is it lawful for a man to put away his wife for every cause?" (v. 3). Jesus answered that, since God joins married persons, man must not separate them: "what therefore God hath joined together, let not man put asunder" (v. 6). In other words, Jesus prohibited divorce. Then, the Pharisees sprung their trap. Moses had said that they could divorce: "They say unto him, Why did Moses then command to give a writing of divorcement, and to put her away?" (v. 7). They referred, of course, to Deuteronomy 24:1–4. Their argument is plain. Moses was the great prophet and lawgiver of God. Jesus stands in opposition to Moses on the matter of the permissibility of divorce. Therefore, Jesus cannot be of God.

The importance of Deuteronomy 24:1–4 for the subject of divorce requires that we look closely at the passage. The regulation concerning divorce found in the passage was grossly misunderstood in the days of Jesus and is still commonly misunderstood today. By this misunderstanding we compound the problem of the apparent lack of agreement between Jesus and Moses, between the New Testament and the Old Testament, and we fail to see the basic agreement between them on this matter of divorce. Our mistake is that we take the regulation as an approval of divorce and even of remarriage. So we understand the words, "let him write her a bill of divorcement, and give it in her hand, and send her out of his house. And when she is departed out of his house, she may go and be another man's wife" (vv. 1–2). We view it as a legitimizing of divorce for an insignificant reason "because he hath found some uncleanness in her" (v. 1). In fact, however, there is in the passage no approval of divorce whatsoever, much less of remarriage. Moses did not here *require* divorce. Nor did he *approve* divorce. But, as Christ pointed out in Matthew 19:8, he "suffered," or permitted, divorce. To suffer something is fundamentally different from approving it. Moses gave Israel a law in Deuteronomy 24 that prescribed what a man had to do if he intended to divorce his wife. Moses took note that men in Israel were divorcing their wives and that they would continue to do so in the future. In such cases they must write out and give to their wives a "writing of cutting off," an official bill of divorce. Moses did not command Israelite men, "Divorce your wives," not even if there was uncleanness in them. But his command was this: *If you are going to divorce your wife, you must give her a bill of divorce."* The purpose of the requirement of giving a bill of divorce was the welfare of the woman who was put away. The woman in Israel was completely subject to the man and entirely at his mercy. If Moses had not required that the husband give a bill of divorce to the woman whom he was determined to put away, the women in Israel would soon have become mere playthings and would have been regarded as little different from whores. The bill of divorce had to be written to her and given in "her hand" (v. 1); that is, it was for her benefit.

There is something else in Deuteronomy 24, often missed, which indicates that Moses did not approve divorce or remarriage, much less command it, but merely suffered it. According to the correct reading of this passage, the regulation made by Moses is that a woman who has been divorced from her original husband and who has married another man may not return to her original husband in case the second man also divorces her. In verses 1–3 Moses merely takes note of what he actually sees happening in Israel. Men are divorcing their wives because of some uncleanness. These divorced women are marrying other men. Then the women are divorced by their second husbands. In such cases Moses forbids a return to the first husband (v. 4). Verses 1–3 do not set forth what Moses approves, but merely what he observes taking place. The translation in the King James Bible is somewhat misleading, especially in verses 1–2, where it leaves the impression that Moses expressly approves of a man's divorcing his wife and even of her remarriage. The correct translation is this:

> When a man hath taken a wife, and married her, and it come to pass that she find no favor in his eyes, because he hath found some uncleanness in her: and he writes her a bill of divorcement and gives it in her hand, and sends her out of his house; and when she is departed out of his house, she goes and becomes another man's wife; and if the latter husband hate her...Her former husband, which sent her away, may not take her again.

According to this translation, it still is an implied requirement that a husband give a bill of divorce to the wife he intends to divorce. But this translation makes clear that Moses is only suffering divorce, not approving it.

It must also be noted that the only ground for the divorce that is suffered by Moses is "some uncleanness." Literally verse 1 reads: "the nakedness of a thing." The phrase occurs elsewhere in scripture, only in Deuteronomy 23:14, which makes it difficult to say exactly what the phrase means. There can be no doubt that the reference is to some kind of sexual pollution or shamefulness in the woman. It is not adultery, for adultery was punishable by death. But it is related to adultery inasmuch as it is sexual uncleanness of some sort. Therefore, it is not the case that Deuteronomy 24 suffered divorce for minor reasons. On the contrary, even in suffering divorce, the Old Testament rigorously restricted divorce to instances that involved impurity in the realm of sex. Thus the Old Testament showed its basic harmony with the teaching of Jesus, who limits divorce to cases of adultery.

Nevertheless, this regulation of Moses in Deuteronomy 24 is unsatisfactory. This is the plain implication of Jesus' words in Matthew 5:31–32: "It hath been said…But I say." Jesus contrasts his teaching, which is the pure truth, with Moses' teaching in Deuteronomy 24. Moses' regulation is unsatisfactory in that Moses tolerated the practice of divorce on a ground other than adultery, as well as tolerating remarriage. Note well, however, that Christ does not blame Moses. Rather, he blames *Israel!* For in Matthew 19:8 he says, "Moses *because of the hardness of your hearts* suffered you to put away your wives" [emphasis added].

This may present a problem regarding the harmony of the Old and New Testaments. In fact, it does present a problem. However, the problem is not this: how can something be right in the Old Testament and wrong in the New Testament? Rather, the problem is this: how can the Old Testament occasionally suffer, or tolerate, the wrong, whereas the New Testament does not suffer it? Polygamy in the Old Testament falls into the same category. Regardless of this problem, it is crystal clear and indisputable that New Testament Christians may never appeal to Deuteronomy 24 in order to apply that Old Testament regulation to their lives. If they do, they acknowledge that they are hard-hearted, just as was the Israel for whom the rule had to be made. Still more, they would thus show that they insist on being hard-hearted. This is the spiritual condition of being ruled by unbelief for Jesus says that "because of the hardness of your hearts," Moses made the rule of Deuteronomy 24.

Between us and Deuteronomy 24 stands the word of Jesus Christ: "But I say!" Christ has abrogated the sufferance of Deuteronomy 24. Divorce for any reason except adultery is suffered no longer. In Jesus Christ the kingdom of heaven has come in its fullness, also regarding the truth of marriage. Within this fully-come kingdom, it stands that "whosoever shall put away his wife, saving for the cause of fornication, causeth her to commit adultery" (Matt. 5:32).

Old Testament Law on Divorce

Yet, Deuteronomy 24 was not the law of the Old Testament on divorce. Deuteronomy 24 was a deviation from the Old Testament law. This is evident from its being a suffering of divorce. One does not suffer what is right and good. One suffers what is not right and not good: a deviation from the law.

In suffering what was wrong, Deuteronomy 24 also suffered much misery in Israel. This is often forgotten by those who are eager to apply the passage to themselves in the hope of relief from a marital problem. In this regulation of Deuteronomy 24 is Moses' warning of the opening up of a most shameful mess and bitter woe. It is possible that a woman goes from one divorce to another and ends up wanting to go back to her first husband. This is the description of a marital mess and of widespread misery. And what about the children who result along the way? The way of a hard heart is the way of misery, already in this life. The same was true in the Old Testament as the result of polygamy. Also that violation of marriage led to trouble for the guilty. We in the New Testament are spared from this misery by the better light on marriage.

Deuteronomy 24 was not the law regarding divorce, but a deviation from the law. The law concerning divorce was that implied in God's institution of marriage in Genesis 2. This is what Jesus called to the attention of the Pharisees in Matthew 19:8. After noting that Deuteronomy 24 was Moses' suffering a deviation from the law of divorce, he reminded the Pharisees: "But from the beginning it was not so." The law concerning divorce is found in Genesis 2:18–25, the record of God's institution of marriage in the beginning. This is the law in both the Old and New Testaments: "What therefore God hath joined together, let not man put asunder" (Matt. 19:6). God joins married persons. Divorce, therefore, is prohibited. God hated divorce also in the Old Testament. He made this clear in Malachi 2:15–16: "Take heed to your spirit, and let none deal treacherously against the wife of his youth. For the LORD, the God of Israel, saith that he hateth putting away." In Matthew 5, therefore, Jesus does not contradict the Old Testament law concerning divorce, but he uncovers it, sets it forth, and shows its full significance: divorce is forbidden.

The Wickedness of Divorce

It must be stressed that Jesus treats divorce in Matthew 5:31–32. He condemns and forbids the putting away of a wife. It is not remarriage that is his concern here, but divorce. There is reason to fear that, although remarriage still shocks us, we become hardened to divorce. If this is so, we need to listen carefully to the Lord.

Neither is it the case that he forbids divorce only because of the possibility of remarriage, as if divorce itself were not sinful. Jesus does indeed point to the possibility of remarriage when divorce occurs. But he condemns divorce, not because it may lead to another evil but because it is itself evil. Whoever divorces his wife sins by virtue of the fact that he divorces her.

Although Jesus condemns divorce in the form of the husband's divorcing his wife, implied is the equal sinfulness of the wife's divorcing her husband. In the days of Jesus, the man had the upper hand, so that whatever divorcing was done was done by the man. Today the woman has the upper hand so that she dominates in the matter of divorce. It is not important who does the divorcing, whether man or woman, but the deed that is committed.

Christ's condemnation of divorce must be understood as a condemnation of all forms of the separation of a man and his wife. He spoke of "putting away." This refers to a legal, official divorce. But it also covers what we know as a suit for separate maintenance. It includes, as well, the simple leaving of one's marriage partner, whether the husband's leaving the wife or the wife's leaving the husband. Putting away, separating, leaving—all these activities come down to the breaking up into two of that which God has made one and which must remain one.

It may happen that the time comes when the wife must leave her husband temporarily, or request her husband to leave. Maybe he gets drunk and beats her and the children. It is not safe for her life and limb that he be in the house with her. Then, although she does not intend to divorce him in the full, official sense, she sees to it that they live apart. But even this is a deadly serious matter. The church must regard it as such. The married persons themselves must regard it as most serious. It is simply an intolerable state of affairs.

Divorce is forbidden in terms of what may happen to the divorced person. To put away one's mate is sin, and one aspect of the sin is the exposure of the other to adultery. Christ says, "Whosoever shall put away his wife...causeth her to commit adultery" (Matt. 5:32). The Lord knows human nature, not only fallen human nature but also human nature as originally created: "It is not good that the man should be alone" (Gen. 2:18). The man who puts his wife away by an official divorce is responsible for putting her in a position where she is tempted to remarry, and this remarriage is adultery according to Christ's words in the last part of Matthew 5:32: "Whosoever shall marry her that is divorced committeth adultery." Or the divorced woman is tempted to commit adultery without remarrying. The man who puts his wife away by separating or by leaving her is also guilty of making her commit adultery. He exposes her to the danger of wicked relationships with other men. This is vividly illustrated in the history of Abram and Sarai in Genesis 12. Abram put away his wife for the sake of his own safety, and she was soon taken into the house of Pharaoh and threatened with an adulterous union with him. God stands for no foolishness in his institution of marriage. Of course, the same holds for the wife who puts her husband away or leaves him. Then she makes him commit adultery. The person who is put away should not commit adultery, not even if she is wickedly divorced. If she does, she is guilty of sin. The last part of verse 32 teaches this. But the partner who did the divorcing will also be to blame. God holds him responsible.

That Jesus forbids divorce in terms of the very real evil, adultery, which in all likelihood results from divorce, may not obscure the truth that the act of divorce is itself sin. No matter whether it results in the other's remarriage or not, altogether apart from any consequences, divorce is sin. The reason is that man in proud rebellion is separating what God has joined together. Man may not loose what God has tied. Marriage is a divine institution. In marriage God makes two, one. It is wrong that the one becomes two again, apart now from the question whether this is even possible. Whether these separated people then try to make new bonds or not, there may be no loosing.

This is the force of Jesus' words on divorce in Matthew 19:4–6:

4. Have ye not read, that he which made them at the beginning made them male and female,

5. And said, For this cause shall a man leave father and mother, and shall cleave to his wife: and they twain shall be one flesh?

6. Wherefore they are no more twain, but one flesh.
What therefore God hath joined together, let not man
put asunder.

That this underlies Jesus' prohibition of divorce also in Matthew 5, the last phrase of verse 32 shows. It is not enough to forbid divorce, but he must add that if the wronged and divorced woman remarries, she and her new husband are guilty of adultery. Why? Because the marriage bond stands, come what may. In condemning divorce Jesus is defending the marriage bond. Because marriage is God's union of a man and woman into one flesh, divorce is forbidden.

One Biblical Ground for Divorce

There is one exception to the forbidding of divorce. That exception is adultery on the part of one's mate: "saving for the cause of fornication" (Matt. 5:32). If a man's wife is unfaithful to him, if she has sexual relations with another man, he may put her away without incurring the wrath of God or the discipline of the church. Adultery is a ground for divorce before God. A husband may divorce his wife on the ground of her adultery, or the wife her husband. He does not have to divorce her, however. Even adultery can be covered by the blood of Christ so that the two remain one flesh in marriage. If by the grace of God the unfaithful wife repents of her adultery, the Christian man can and should forgive her and take her back. Likewise, God has often forgiven and taken back his wife, Israel-church, after she has played the whore with many idols. Yet the adultery of the wife may be such that it makes life together impossible.

Here we see the seriousness of adultery. Adultery is taken lightly today. The world builds comedies around it in the movies and on television. Popular novels treat it in a frivolous manner and even glorify it. Even in the church jokes about it are heard. Christ does not take adultery lightly! In the fact that adultery, and adultery only, is of such a nature that it separates what God has joined together, you see the seriousness and dreadfulness of this sin. By its very nature, adultery strikes at the heart of marriage: the intimacy of two, the becoming one flesh of the man and his wife.

When Jesus forbids divorce, "saving for the cause of fornication," he teaches that there is only one ground for divorce. Only adultery breaks the marriage bond to the degree that the husband and the wife may be apart, loosed from one life in one home, at one table, and in one bed. Nothing else is a ground for divorce, nothing else whatever. In a world of sin and death, there are many evils that may trouble marriage: insanity, paralysis, not only husbands who itch for divorce, but also brawling wives who are miserable to live with. But none of these evils is ground for divorce. This is the meaning of the phrases in the marriage vow that state, "for better for worse, for richer, for poorer, in sickness and in health...till death us do part."[1]

No husband should have ground to complain that the church forbids divorce, but allows his wife to go on being a shrew. No wife should complain that although it forbids her to divorce her husband, the church allows her husband to be a brute. For the church also demands that husbands and wives carry out their marital responsibilities, as noted in previous chapters. And the church must back up her preaching with discipline. Not only does our Lord admonish believers to live together, but he also admonishes them to live together properly, in love and peace.

---

1 "A Classical [Marriage] Service," in Perry H. Biddle, Jr., *A Marriage Manual* (Grand Rapids, MI: Wm. B. Eerdmans Publishing Co., 1994), 109–10.

The law forbidding divorce holds for every married man and woman, the unbeliever as well as the believer. "Whosoever shall put away his wife" (Matt. 5:32) sins. This is the law for marriage, all marriage, "from the beginning" (Matt. 19:4). How depraved is the world! How ripe for judgment is our society!

Christ Who Does Not Divorce

Christ directed his word on divorce, however, to the citizens of the kingdom of heaven, that is, to the believing church. It is part of the Sermon on the Mount. It is for believers who receive it by God's grace. It is for those whose hearts have been regenerated by the Spirit to love God and, in thankfulness for salvation, to honor his institution of marriage. Believers see this word of Jesus against divorce as a testimony to his own faithfulness to his bride, the church. Christ upholds marriage as the mystery of himself and the church. He never puts his people away, although by their sins they have given him ample cause. This faithfulness of love believers are called to reflect in their marriages.

8

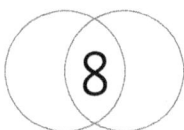

The Marriage of Believer and Unbeliever

And unto the married I command, yet not I, but the Lord, Let not the wife depart from her husband: But and if she depart, let her remain unmarried, or be reconciled to her husband: and let not the husband put away his wife. But to the rest speak I, not the Lord: If any brother hath a wife that believeth not, and she be pleased to dwell with him, let him not put her away. And the woman which hath an husband that believeth not, and if he be pleased to dwell with her, let her not leave him. For the unbelieving husband is sanctified by the wife, and the unbelieving wife is sanctified by the husband: else were your children unclean; but now are they holy. But if the unbelieving depart, let him depart. A brother or a sister is not under bondage in such cases: but God hath called us to peace. For what knowest thou, O wife, whether thou shalt save thy husband? or how knowest thou, O man, whether thou shalt save thy wife? But as God hath distributed to every man, as the Lord hath called every one, so let him walk. And, so ordain I in all churches. —1 Corinthians 7:10–17

In 1 Corinthians 7:10–17 Paul answers two distinct questions that were raised by members of the Corinthian church and gives instruction concerning two distinct marriage problems that were found in that congregation. Throughout Chapter 7, the apostle is replying to questions which believers in Corinth sent to him. Verse 1 shows this: "Now concerning the things whereof ye wrote unto me." These were questions concerning marriage. In verses 10–17 Paul addresses two different problems faced by saints in Corinth and brought up by them in their questions about marriage. Verses 10–11 are Paul's instructions for one group of people with regard to their specific problem. Verses 12–16 are his instructions for another group with regard to their different problem in marriage.

One difference between the two admonitions is that the first is the Lord's command, whereas the second is Paul's command. Verse 10 reads, "And unto the married I command, yet not I, but the Lord." Verse 12 reads, "But to the rest speak I, not the Lord." It is a mistake to take this to mean that the first admonition is a divine order which we must obey whereas the second is merely Paul's personal advice which we may take or leave as we please. Both of these admonitions are divine commands which we are required to obey. That the second admonition is also an order to be carried out, not merely weak advice, is evident from verse 17: "And so ordain I in all churches." Referring to the instruction he has given in verses 10–16, Paul says that he has ordained things, that is, laid down orders.

The first admonition is Paul's restatement of a teaching that Jesus himself ("the Lord" [v. 10]) explicitly made while he was on earth. Jesus himself commanded his people not to divorce or leave their mates and never to remarry. The contents of verses 10–11 are simply the commands of Jesus as found in Matthew 5:31–32 and in Matthew 19:9. The second admonition (1 Cor. 7:12–16), however, is a teaching that Jesus did not have occasion to give while he was on earth, at least not in the specific form required by the circumstances in the church at Corinth.

Therefore Paul, Christ's infallibly guided apostle, gives the necessary instruction. But it is the Lord Jesus who speaks through Paul by his Holy Spirit, and Paul's instruction is based on and is in harmony with the basic principles of marriage laid down by Christ.

The main distinction between the two admonitions is that the first concerns husbands and wives who are both believers, but that the second gives instruction to believers who are married to unbelievers.

The two admonitions are basically one. They are one in that they both are concerned with the truth of marriage, particularly with the believer's calling in marriage. In both admonitions Paul speaks to believers. This does not imply that God does not also demand unbelievers to observe his marriage ordinance, for he certainly does. But the significance of the apostle's addressing believers is that he comes to them with the rule of God for their thankful lives in the world; that the law of marriage he brings is the law of the Lord Jesus whom his people love and desire to serve; and that with the command there is the promise of grace to obey.

The admonitions are also one in that both show the nature of marriage as a lifelong bond of intimate fellowship between a man and his wife. Both bring out the firmness and holiness of the divine institution. This is especially the case with the second admonition, which deals with a special case of marital hardship.

Forbidden to Separate

Paul forbids the wife to leave her husband, but he goes on to stipulate what her calling is in case she does leave. If she departs,

she must "remain unmarried, or be reconciled to her husband"
(1 Cor. 7:11). There may not be any remarriage. The fact that Paul
adds instruction to cover the possibility of a wife's leaving her
husband ("But and if she depart" [v. 11]) does not legitimize her
leaving. The main admonition in verses 10–11 is: do not leave
your mate; do not separate. The woman who leaves her husband
may not appeal to the fact that she is obeying Paul's command
to remain unmarried in order to justify her leaving. Regardless
of the fact that she does not marry someone else, she should not
depart from her husband. The same goes for the husband: "let not
the husband put away his wife" (v. 11). He must not separate from
his wife, whether by putting her away or by leaving her.

In commanding this Paul is only repeating, almost word for
word, what the Lord Jesus Christ taught. This is why Paul writes
in verse 10 that his command is really not his command, but the
Lord's command: "I command, yet not I, but the Lord." In Matthew 5:32 Jesus said, "Whosoever shall put away his wife, saving
for the cause of fornication, causeth her to commit adultery: and
whosoever shall marry her that is divorced committeth adultery."

We cannot help noting once more the amazing strictness of
our calling in marriage. This in turn reminds us how seriously we
must regard marriage, specifically our own marriage. It is not the
making of new marriages that is forbidden, but the mere physical
separation of the husband and wife. Marriage, as the becoming
one flesh of the man and the woman, forbids loosing, departing,
and putting away. God takes our being together in one house and
our sharing one life seriously. God is jealous that this aspect of his
institution be safeguarded.

The prohibition of leaving and putting away in 1 Corinthians
7:10–11 is the simple rule that covers all cases in the church. In a
sinful world there are innumerable complicated situations, also

regarding the marriage of believers, which seem to demand separation at the very least. There are husbands who distress their wives; there are wives who treat their husbands cruelly. Every pastor has had the feeling at some point in his difficult ministry to the married that a marriage should be broken up because of the "irreconcilable differences" between the husband and the wife. But woe to him if he gives such counsel, for the counsel of Christ is: be reconciled with regard to your irreconcilable differences. The rule of Christ is: separation is forbidden.

The church's faithfulness in preaching this rule and enforcing it with discipline will make a great difference in the practical life of the congregation. If the troubled, even fighting, husband and wife realize that separation is no option, they will pray and work to remove the cause of the trouble, to repent and forgive, and to be reconciled. They understand that this is the only way out for them. But if the church opens the door of separation just a crack, motivated no doubt by sympathy for the hard circumstances of some, the result will be that many husbands and wives will choose this alternative as the solution to their problems. It is easier to separate than it is to confess our sins to our mate, to forgive each other, and to strive to put away the sin that estranges us.

Nevertheless, there are times, in the church too, when the wife is simply forced to leave her husband, at least for a time. It may be that he falls into the sin of drunkenness for a time and beats her and the children. It may be that living with him in this sin-cursed world jeopardizes her in some other way, so that leaving is required. There are not many of these cases, but there is the possibility of such a case. In such instances the rule is to "let her remain unmarried, or be reconciled to her husband" (1 Cor. 7:11). The wife must know, right from the start, that remarriage is out. This will serve to act as a check on wives who think they want to leave their husbands, as well as on husbands who think about leaving their wives. It will also serve to encourage wives who have left, to work at being reconciled to their husbands. But if the church opens the door of remarriage to estranged husbands and wives, it is to be expected that unhappy husbands and wives will pour through that door, easily leaving their mates and taking up with others. But scripture has shut that door tightly: "let her remain unmarried, or be reconciled to her husband."

Regarding those few instances of a wife having reason to leave her husband, both she and the church must regard the situation as intolerable and must work to achieve her return in the right way. The church is responsible for working with the separated couple through the pastor and elders. It is to be regretted that sometimes the church is not called on to help until the trouble in the marriage has reached the point of causing separation.

The apostle, however, does not have in view the departing of the believing wife from her husband on the ground of his drunkenness or abuse. Inasmuch as the apostle in verses 10–11 is simply repeating the instruction that the Lord Jesus gave during his earthly ministry, the ground that is in view for the wife's departing is the one ground for divorce that the Lord permitted: fornication. The teaching of the apostle is that the believing wife may not leave her husband. Leaving includes actual separation and formal divorce. This is the rule. Nevertheless, there is a possibility that she does lawfully depart from her husband: "but and if she depart" (v. 11). The Lord Jesus allowed for this in Matthew 5:31–32: "saving for the cause of fornication." If her husband is unfaithful to her by having sexual relations with another, the wife may depart. Even in this case, however, she may not marry another. Her options are only that she "remain unmarried or be reconciled to her husband" (1 Cor. 7:11).

This passage is explicit, conclusive proof that the innocent party in a divorce is forbidden by the Lord and his apostle to remarry.[1]

The Mixed Marriage

After answering the question in 1 Corinthians 7 concerning separation from one's mate, the apostle turns in verses 12–16 to a special case of marital hardship. This special case is that of the marriage of a believer and an unbeliever. Paul speaks in verse 12 of the marriage of a "brother [who] hath a wife that believeth not" and in verse 13 of the marriage of a "woman which hath an husband that believeth not." According to verse 14 the apostle is concerned with marriages in which either the man is an unbelieving husband or the woman is an unbelieving wife. The spiritual condition of one of the two married persons is such that he or she lacks faith in Christ Jesus. It is a condition of spiritual death and ignorance. This person is a natural man, unregenerated, not indwelt by the Holy Spirit. There are in the world two kinds of persons: those having faith and those lacking faith, those possessing the Spirit and those devoid of the Spirit, believers and unbelievers. Now in the marriage under consideration, one of the married persons is an unbeliever. This is not the same as a reprobate, although this person may eventually prove to be a reprobate. We cannot tell whether anyone is a reprobate, at least not until he dies. All that we can know is that a person is a believer or an unbeliever. We know this by his confession and by his walk. Therefore, the "brother" of verse 12, the believing member of the church,

---

1 For a thorough treatment of the crucially important passage—1 Corinthians 7:10–11—see David J. Engelsma, "The Prohibition of the Remarriage of the Innocent Party," in *Better to Marry: Sex and Marriage in 1 Corinthians 6 and 7*, 2nd ed. (Jenison, MI: Reformed Free Publishing Association, 2014), 107–22.

knows that his wife is an unbeliever. He knows this because she says so and because she lives in an unbelieving way. She may be an elect, and, therefore, he hopes to the very end of her life that he may save her (v. 16). But he does not know this and cannot know this. All he knows is that she is an unbeliever.

Paul finds it necessary to say something about such marriages. Saints in Corinth raised questions to their apostle about such marriages, because some members of the Corinthian church had such marriages. That there were marriages in Corinth in which one was a believer and the other an unbeliever is understandable. The church at Corinth was recently established. The saints there were recently called out of darkness into God's marvelous light. The believers were recently regenerated, converted, and given faith. Before their conversion they had married, and, of course, they had married unbelievers like themselves. Then the gospel came. For some the coming of the gospel had the result that the husband was converted and believed, but the wife remained in her spiritual death and unbelief. Or the wife was converted, but the husband rejected Christ in the gospel. Finding themselves in such circumstances, the believing members of such marriages cried out to Paul, "What must we think of our marriage? What must we do?"

It was not so with the Corinthian Christians that they had disobediently married unbelievers after the gospel came and after they believed. This is forbidden by the word of God in 1 Corinthians 7:39, where the apostle states that believers may marry "only in the Lord." If the trouble of the Corinthian believers of being married to unbelievers had been due to their disobedient disregard for God's command not to date and marry unbelievers, Paul might have answered them, "Well, you made your bed; now sleep in it, asking God for the grace to endure the chastisement he sends you." But the predicament of the Corinthian Christians was not of their own willful doing. It was part of the inescapable evil of this present time. It was one instance of the misery to which also the elect children of God are exposed in our sinful world.

In this world of darkness, men blindly stumble into evil, and that evil can have consequences of lifelong sorrow. But the institutions and laws of God are never bent and twisted to fit the perverse circumstances of fallen man. Man is to blame for this dark, wretched, woeful world. The doctrine of original sin teaches that every man is to blame for this. God will not cease being a holy and righteous God because man has become blind, foolish, and evil. Also for believers, the way out of predicaments, grievous though they be, is never the way of denying God, compromising his righteousness, or changing his law. Specifically, the answer to hard problems in marriage may not be the adjustment of God's institution of marriage to suit us.

One can certainly sympathize with the anguished questions of the Corinthians who found themselves in such marriages. For the believing mate the marriage was filled with hardship. Righteousness and unrighteousness, light and darkness, Christ and Belial lived together in the same house, at the same board, and in the same bed. At the very least there was disharmony; perhaps there was open hatred and persecution. And it was the believer who was regarded (with some right) as being responsible for the trouble. Before the believer's conversion, all went well. Both were one in their unbelief and idolatry. Then the believer changed. Christ brought the sword of division between those of one household. From that time on, the tensions of the antithesis were felt in all the life of the believing man and his unbelieving wife. In all his life the believer walked toward God; in all her life the unbeliever walked away from God.

Still more, it is likely from Paul's remarks in 1 Corinthians 7:14 (concerning the unbeliever being sanctified by the believer) that the believing member of the marriage feared that it might even be sinful to continue to live with the unbeliever. The believer reasoned like this: "There is no spiritual fellowship between us. Therefore, what fellowship is there at all? Is not the intimacy of married life a danger to me? Will I not be defiled by my unbelieving and wicked wife? Is it not always the case that friendship between a believer and an unbeliever corrupts the believer and makes him unclean?"

By no means ought we to minimize the hardship of such a marriage. The spiritual fellowship that believers have in Christ is the heart of the communion of marriage. At best the marriage of a believer and an unbeliever means a life of trouble and heartache for the believer. No wonder that these believers wrote Paul, asking about such marriages and about their calling in them.

A Valid Marriage

Paul's answer was his insistence that such a marriage is a real and valid marriage. He commands the believer to live with the unbeliever in the bond of marriage: "Let him [the believing husband] not put her [the unbelieving wife] away" (1 Cor. 7:12); "let her [a believing wife] not leave him [an unbelieving husband]" (v. 13). The simple reason for this command is that the believer and the unbeliever are truly married. Although the man is an unbeliever, he is the believer's husband (v. 13); although the woman is an unbeliever, she is the believer's wife (v. 12). If they were not truly married, the apostle's command to them to live together would be wicked, for only married people may live together.

The validity of the marriage of a believer and an unbeliever is due to the fact that marriage is an institution of God in the sphere of creation. We must be careful not to misunderstand what it means that marriage is a symbol of Christ and the church. This does not mean that marriage is only valid within the church of Jesus Christ, within the realm of grace. It does not mean that for a marriage to be a genuine marriage God's grace must be present in both the husband and the wife. God's grace is necessary for two people to fulfill the idea of marriage and for them to carry out the calling of husbands and wives in marriage. But altogether apart from God's grace, a valid marriage is certainly possible, because marriage is an ordinance of God in the realm of creation.

There are some institutions of God that exist only in the church. One of these is the institution of the Lord's supper. If a group of unbelievers in the world try to celebrate the supper, they fail in the sense that what they have is not the Lord's supper, even though outwardly everything resembles what is done in the church. Outside of the church there is no sacrament and can be no sacrament.

But there are also institutions of God that exist outside the sphere of the church, within the sphere of creation. An example is the institution of civil government. The state is an institution of God that exists and functions outside the realm of the church. An unbeliever, devoid of God's grace, may be king or president, truly king or president, so that believers are called to honor him and obey him as "the minister of God" (Rom. 13:4). Although he is an unbeliever, even a reprobate, he is put in his office by God, functions validly in that office, and must be honored by us for his office's sake and the Lord's sake.

So it is with the institution of marriage. God instituted marriage in paradise, prior to the fall, prior to a redeemed church, and prior to the redeeming grace of Jesus Christ. Therefore, when unbelievers marry, apart from grace, they are validly married, not only in the eyes of the state but also in the eyes of God. If these unbelievers should commit adultery, God's wrath falls on them for a very real violation of a real marriage. Also, two people do not need to be married in a church building, in a church service, or by a minister in order to be genuinely married. We urge the young people of the church to be married by the minister, preferably in a service of divine worship,[2] but not because this is the only valid marriage.

Since marriage is an ordinance of God in the sphere of creation, whenever two people marry, God joins them together and makes them one flesh, even though he may be angry with them for their godless, unrighteous motives. This is the case whenever two unbelievers marry. They do not marry in the fear of God. For this God is angry with them. Yet he joins them together, and they are married. The same thing is true when an unbeliever takes

---

2 An early rendition of article 70 of the Church Order of Dordt reads as follows: "Since it is proper that the matrimonial state be confirmed in the presence of Christ's Church, according to the Form for that purpose, the Consistories shall attend to it" (Idzerd Van Dellen and Martin Monsma, *The Church Order Commentary* [Grand Rapids, MI: Zondervan Publishing House, 1941], 286). For the defense of consistories' encouraging their members to have their marriages confirmed in worship services of the church, see Van Dellen and Monsma, *Church Order Commentary*, 286–90. In 2000 the synod of the Protestant Reformed Churches revised article 70 of the Church Order. The article now reads in part as follows: "The consistories shall see to it that those who marry, marry in the Lord, whether it be in a private ceremony or in an official worship service" (Article 33, in *Acts of Synod...of the Protestant Reformed Churches in America 2000*, 45). What is added in the newly revised article allows the officiating minister to use or not to use the "adopted [Reformed] form" for marriage as he or the marrying couple wishes, if the marriage is not confirmed in the presence of Christ's church. This explains the recent proliferation of forms at marriage ceremonies that differ widely, and usually not for the better, from the "adopted [Reformed] form." Most of them manage to omit the opening line of the adopted form with its sober, but thoroughly and importantly realistic, to say nothing of Reformed, acknowledgment that "married persons are generally, by reason of sin, subject to many troubles and afflictions."

office in the government. He does not enter the presidency in the consciousness that God has set him up on high or with the desire to serve God in that office. In fact, he has evil motives: his fame, his power, and his wealth. Yet it is God who puts him in that office and who vests him with authority so that he is really president. In this light we must understand Jesus' words in Matthew 19:6: "What therefore God hath joined together, let not man put asunder." Whenever two persons make use of God's institution of marriage, regardless of their spiritual condition, God joins them together. Therefore, man is forbidden to separate them.

All of this is plain from Paul's instruction in 1 Corinthians 7:12–16 to believers who are married to unbelievers.

God joined them in marriage when they were both unbelievers. Therefore, even though later one became a believer while the other remained an unbeliever, they are still validly married and must live together as husband and wife. Although the one may prove ultimately to be a reprobate by dying in unbelief, the marriage is a valid marriage.

However, only the believer is able to do the will of God regarding marriage, for only he has the Holy Spirit and grace of God. One aspect of the will of God for marriage is the command given to the believer who has an unbelieving mate: maintain the marriage! The will of God for the believer who has an unbelieving wife is, "let him not put her away" (v. 12). The will of God for the believer who has an unbelieving husband is, "let her not leave him" (v. 13).

The basis of this command is simply that the two people are married, and marriage is a lifelong bond. The apostle expresses the basis of all his instruction concerning marriage in 1 Corinthians 7:39: "The wife is bound by the law as long as her husband liveth; but if her husband be dead, she is at liberty to be married to whom she will; only in the Lord."

Encouragement of the Believer

Paul adds two considerations to encourage believers with unbelieving mates to heed his command to maintain their marriages. The first consideration is that given in 1 Corinthians 7:14: "For the unbelieving husband is sanctified by the wife, and the unbelieving wife is sanctified by the husband: else were your children unclean; but now are they holy."

With these words Paul deals with the fear of the believing member of the marriage that he will be defiled by his fellowship with his unbelieving wife. This fear is understandable. Ordinarily, friendship between a believer and an unbeliever results in the corrupting of the believer. Therefore, God has always warned his people against friendship with the world. It is not surprising that the believer married to an unbeliever anxiously wondered whether he should not break up the marriage, lest he be contaminated. But Paul lays that fear to rest. Although ordinarily it is true that fellowship of a believer and an unbeliever corrupts the believer, in the marriage of a believer and an unbeliever the opposite will be true: the unbeliever will be sanctified by the believer. This cannot mean that the unbeliever is cleansed from sin and consecrated to God in heartfelt love, for he is and remains an unbeliever. The unbeliever is sanctified only regarding his position as marriage partner of the believer. The prevailing principle in the marriage of a believer and an unbeliever is not the impurity of the unbeliever, but the holiness of the believer. Of course, this presupposes that the believer walks in holiness in the marriage. This peculiar sanctification of the unbeliever in his association with his believing wife is not for his benefit, but for the benefit of the believer who is married to him. The purpose of the Holy Spirit is to safeguard the believer from being defiled by the unbeliever, both regarding her person and her marriage in all its aspects.

Covenant Children

The proof of this unique holiness of the fellowship of a believer and an unbeliever in marriage is the holiness of the children who result from their union: "else were your children unclean; but now are they holy" (1 Cor. 7:14). The holiness of the children is evidence that the holiness of the believer, not the wickedness of the unbeliever, determines the spiritual character of the marriage. Just as is the case with the children of two believing parents, the children of one believing parent are also included in God's covenant. Redemption from sin by the blood of Christ, and the Holy Spirit, the author of faith, are promised to them.[3] They are "sanctified in Christ."[4] Therefore, they must be baptized and reared in the fear of the Lord.

Holiness does not necessarily characterize every child of one believing parent any more than it characterizes every child of two believing parents. When scripture calls our children holy and promises salvation to them, it speaks organically, with reference to the elect children of believers. "The children of the promise are counted for the seed" (Rom. 9:8). But God does establish his covenant in the line of the generations of a believer married to an unbeliever and promises to save that believer's children, even though one of the parents is an unbeliever. This is encouragement to the believer to maintain her marriage to an unbeliever.

Saving the Unbeliever

The second motive that a believer has for maintaining his marriage to an unbeliever is given in 1 Corinthians 7:16: "For what

---

3   Heidelberg Catechism A 74, in Philip Schaff, ed., *The Creeds of Christendom with a History and Critical Notes*, 6th ed., 3 vols. (New York: Harper and Row, 1931; repr., Grand Rapids, MI: Baker Books, 2007), 3:417.

4   This is the description of the children of believing parents in the Reformed Form for the Administration of Baptism, in *Confessions and Church Order*, 260.

knowest thou, O wife, whether thou shalt save thy husband? or how knowest thou, O man, whether thou shalt save thy wife?" The apostle holds before the believer the possibility that the Holy Spirit may save the unbelieving mate through the sanctified life of the believer. It may very well happen that the unbeliever is sanctified by the believer in the full, rich sense of the word. Peter also speaks of this striking working of God in marriages of believers and unbelievers: "Likewise, ye wives, be in subjection to your own husbands; that, if any obey not the word, they also may without the word be won by the conversation of the wives; While they behold your chaste conversation coupled with fear" (1 Pet. 3:1–2). God gives the believer no absolute guarantee that this will occur, but he does allow the believer to have the hope that he will save his mate. And this hope is an incentive to the believer to continue to live with the unbeliever right up to the moment of his death, always having the hope that he will be saved.

Desertion

There is, however, also the possibility that the unbeliever is not willing to live with his believing wife or with her believing husband. It may happen that the holiness of Christ in the believer enrages the unbeliever and repulses him so that he leaves. Paul treats this problem in 1 Corinthians 7:15: "But if the unbelieving depart, let him depart. A brother or a sister is not under bondage in such cases: but God hath called us to peace." Some suppose they have found in this text another biblical ground for divorce, and some even try to find in it a biblical ground for remarriage. They call this ground "willful desertion." But to find in verse 15 a biblical ground for either divorce or remarriage is a very serious and a very foolish error.

First, we do well to remind ourselves, that the believer may never take the initiative in breaking up a marriage with an unbeliever, whether by putting him away or by leaving him. Verse 15 may not be read in such a way that it flies in the face of the apostle's express prohibition of a believer divorcing his unbelieving mate. Verse 15 does not speak of any action on the part of the believer. It speaks rather of the action of the unbeliever: he departs. All that the believer does is to acquiesce in the leaving of the unbeliever: "let him depart."

Second, it is a very poor and dangerous business to base such a weighty matter as a new ground for divorce and a new ground for remarriage on this one text, which does not even mention divorce, much less remarriage. Nowhere else in scripture are there any passages that teach that willful desertion is either a ground for divorce or a dissolving of the marriage bond that allows a believer to remarry. On the contrary, the scriptures elsewhere explicitly teach that there is only one ground for divorce, namely, the "fornication" of one's mate (Matt. 5:32; 19:9). If Paul here adds another ground for divorce, he contradicts the teaching of Jesus Christ. Elsewhere, scripture teaches, as plainly as could ever be desired, that only death dissolves the marriage bond so that one may marry again. This is Paul's own doctrine in 1 Corinthians 7:39 and in Romans 7:1–3. If Paul teaches in verse 15 of the Corinthians passage that also desertion dissolves a marriage and is a ground for remarriage, he contradicts himself.

The text is not teaching that the desertion of the unbeliever is a ground for divorce. Allowing an unbelieving mate to depart is quite different from divorcing him. And even if it were true that the text did teach that desertion is a ground for divorce, there is not so much as a hint in the text that remarriage is permitted. The apostle has already taught that the woman who finds it necessary to live apart from her husband must "remain unmarried, or be reconciled to her husband" (v. 11). And in verse 39 he says that married people are bound to each other for life and that only death gives liberty to be married to another.

Spiritual Peace

The text speaks only of the spiritual peace of the believer when her unbelieving husband wickedly deserts her. "Let him depart" (1 Cor. 7:15) means that in your heart, in your mind, with your will, and in your emotions, accept that departure and the shattering of your marriage with peace. Nor need you run to and fro in the earth all the rest of your life to try to force the unbeliever back. Let him go.

What this letting go consists of is explained by the words "a brother or a sister is not under bondage in such cases" (v. 15). The Holy Spirit does not say that we are not bound to our mate any more, but that we are not under bondage. Those who find in these words permission for divorce and remarriage apparently confuse "being under bondage" with "being bound." They read the text as if it said, "A brother or a sister is not bound to his mate any more." But these are two entirely different words and two entirely different ideas. If they are the same, all married men are not only bound to their wives, but are also in bondage to their wives. The Greek word for being bound is *deo*. This word is used in verse 39, where the apostle says that we are bound to our mates until death parts us. The Greek word for being under bondage is *douloo*. This is the word used in verse 15: "A brother or a sister is not under bondage." Being under bondage is the condition of spiritual slavery. One is in this miserable condition if he lives in the guilt of his sin.

Still Bound

Even though one's mate deserts her, the two are bound in the marriage bond. This is why the deserter is held accountable by God for his wicked desertion and why, in case he takes up with another woman, God will punish him for adultery. But if the unbeliever departs, the believer is not under bondage; that is, there is no need for her to feel guilt and shame at not living with her God-given mate. She is not enslaved by sin's guilt. As she contemplates her peculiar status as a married woman not living with her husband, she may be free from all fear and worry that stem from sinning against God's marriage word.

That this is the meaning of the apostle's words "not under bondage" is evident also from the words that immediately follow: "but God hath called us to peace" (1 Cor. 7:15). These words state the opposite of that expressed in the words "not under bondage." If the apostle had meant that the believer is not bound any more to the deserting mate, he would have written, "but God now gives you the right to divorce your husband and marry another" or "but now the brother or sister has the right to marry somebody else." But he writes no such thing. Rather, he says, "but God hath called us to peace." Although you have been deserted and, therefore, live alone, separated from your lawful husband or wife, instead of having an enslaved, fearful, and despondent conscience, you may have, and by God's calling do have, a heart and mind that are at peace. You are at peace with God; you are at peace regarding your shattered marriage; you are at peace with your earthly life. Now, as God has distributed to you, as the Lord has called you, so walk (v. 17).

"I Can Do All Things"

Strong words these are to recent converts, practical words on marriage that are governed by the lofty principle of Ephesians 5:31–32 that marriage is the mystery of Christ and the church. But they are not words that are impossible for the saints to practice, not even the saints in a special case of marital hardship, for the grace of Jesus Christ enables us to do them.

Let no wife whose believing husband is a weak and sinful man say, "I cannot live with him any longer." Let no wife who must leave her husband say, "I cannot remain unmarried." Let no husband or wife with an unbelieving mate say, "I cannot stand to live with that infidel anymore." Let no husband or wife whose unbelieving mate forsakes him or her say, "It is impossible for me to live a single life." Difficult and painful as the apostle's ordinances may be for the saint, he knows that it is God who has distributed to him the marital circumstances of his life and that it is the Lord Jesus who calls him to live righteously in those circumstances (1 Cor. 7:17). God never gives his child a greater burden than he can bear; Christ never calls him to do anything without also giving sufficient grace. In this peace "so let him walk" (v. 17).

9

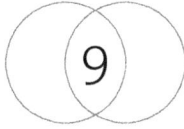

The Unbreakable Marriage Bond

And I say unto you, Whosoever shall put away his wife, except it
be for fornication, and shall marry another, commiteth adultery:
and whoso marrieth her which is put away doth commit adultery.
—Matthew 19:9

Jesus' teaching on marriage in Matthew 19:9 was occasioned by a tempting question of the Pharisees. "The Pharisees also came unto him, tempting him, and saying unto him, Is it lawful for a man to put away his wife for every cause?" (v. 3). In Israel at that time, there were two different opinions about the lawful grounds for divorce. The stricter party held that divorce was permissible only on the ground of the wife's adultery. The looser party held that almost any dissatisfaction that a husband might have with his wife was sufficient ground for divorce. One member of this party made the wife's burning of her husband's meal a ground for divorce. Another said that the mere fact that a man found another woman more beautiful than his wife was ground for divorce. To this view of the looser party the Pharisees refer when they speak of divorce for every cause. But the Pharisees were not sincerely seeking after the truth. They were tempting Jesus. Jesus was supposed to choose one or the other of the two positions on divorce and thus entangle himself in the prevailing controversy.

The Lord's reply was a refusal to choose either of the alternatives found among the Jews. Rather, he chose God's position on divorce as set forth in the original institution of marriage in Genesis 2:18–25. That position, as well as the force of Jesus' answer to the Pharisees in Matthew 19:4–6, is the absolute prohibition of divorce: "Wherefore they are no more twain, but one flesh. What therefore God hath joined together, let not man put asunder" (v. 6).

Although surprised by this answer, the Pharisees were not yet defeated. It might still be possible to trap him, for Jesus has apparently contradicted the great Old Testament prophet and lawgiver Moses, who in Deuteronomy 24:1 commanded "let him write her a bill of divorcement, and give it in her hand, and send her out of his house" (see Matt. 19:7). We have already taken note of Jesus' response to the accusation that he contradicts Moses. Moses merely suffered, or permitted, divorce. Moses did this, in spite of God's original prohibition of divorce, because the nation of Israel had hard hearts and would not obey God's law on divorce. But Jesus has come to insist on the original doctrine of marriage and divorce, so that he sets aside even Moses' sufferance. Then, in Matthew 19:9, Jesus gave his own authoritative teaching on marriage, divorce, and remarriage.

We have already considered Jesus' teaching on divorce as given in Matthew 5:31–32. It is not this aspect of Matthew 19:9 that now concerns us. But we are concerned with the possibility of remarriage, which is introduced in this text. Because Matthew 19:9 includes the phrase "and shall marry another," some suppose that married persons whose mates are guilty of fornication are permitted not only to divorce, but also to remarry. The question we face as we consider the text is this: does the Lord Jesus allow remarriage while one's original mate yet lives, specifically the remarriage of one whose mate commits fornication? We will take other New Testament passages into consideration also, but we will learn from this text itself that remarriage is forbidden. Marriage is an unbreakable bond.

The Subject is Divorce

It is important to keep in mind what subject controls the entire passage in Matthew 19 of which verse 9 is a part. It has become common to view verse 9 as giving a biblical ground for remarriage. Since no other New Testament passage suggests such a divine sanction of remarriage while one's original mate is still living, this one text has had to bear all the weight of the argument for remarriage. Discussion of the text usually centers around the question whether it does, in fact, allow for remarriage. The result is that readers assume that the text is dealing mainly with remarriage and approach it from this viewpoint.

In fact, however, the main subject of the text is not remarriage, but divorce. This is the issue in the question of the Pharisees: may a man divorce his wife for every reason? This is the issue in Jesus' answer: "let not man put asunder" (v. 6). This is also the basic issue in verse 9, the climax of the whole passage. Jesus is talking and giving instruction about divorce. He is not addressing himself to the matter of the legitimacy of remarriage. Remarriage enters in only incidentally. There are other passages in which remarriage is on the foreground, but not here. Here the subject is divorce. This is the approach, therefore, that we must take to the text. We must expect to hear what the Lord says about divorce. We must also remember that the thrust of Jesus' words in Matthew 19:9, as in the entire passage, is a rigorous, emphatic prohibition of divorce.

It is true that Jesus makes an exception to this prohibition, just as he does in Matthew 5:31–32: "saving for the cause of fornication." But this may never obscure the overall force of the Lord's instruction concerning divorce: thou shalt not put asunder what God has joined together. How contrary to Jesus' purpose with this instruction that men run to the passage to find easy license for divorce and remarriage! Our spirit must be in harmony with the Lord's spirit as he uttered these words. We must have a spirit that reverences God's institution of marriage as Jesus did and that is appalled by the insolence of those who handle God's ordinance as they please.

May the Innocent Party Remarry?

Even though we recognize that the main subject is divorce, not remarriage, we must face the question whether Matthew 19:9 allows for remarriage. For it does mention remarrying: "whosoever shall put away his wife, except it be for fornication, and shall marry another, committeth adultery."

What does Jesus literally say? A man who divorces his wife, not on the ground of her fornication but for some other reason, and marries another woman, commits adultery. The man's wife has not been guilty of fornication. She has been faithful to him. The ground that he uses to divorce her is probably "mental cruelty." If this man remarries, he is guilty of breaking the seventh commandment of God's law. His life is constant adultery. The explicit teaching of Jesus is a condemnation of remarriage, not an approval of it.

From this teaching, however, some infer that a man whose wife does commit fornication may not only divorce her, but may also remarry. They understand the Lord to permit a man to remarry if his wife has been guilty of fornication with another man. Similarly, a wife is permitted to remarry if her husband has sinned against her by fornication. In such a case one does not commit adultery when he marries another, even though the original mate is still living. Men see an implication in Jesus' words that can be put thus: "whosoever divorces his wife on the ground of her fornication does not commit adultery if he marries another."

The reason for this interpretation by some, of course, is the text's mention of remarriage and the relation that is thought to exist between the words about remarriage and the phrase "except it be for fornication." The Lord refers to the possibility of remarriage: "and shall marry another." It is assumed that the phrase "except it be for fornication" qualifies the words about remarrying. When Jesus says "except for fornication," he certainly is granting one ground for divorce. No one denies this. But those who view the text as permitting remarriage maintain that Jesus' words "except for fornication" also apply to "marrying another," so that Jesus also is granting a ground for remarriage.

If this is the correct interpretation of Matthew 19:9, scripture gives one ground for remarriage, just as it gives one ground for divorce. That one ground is "fornication," the unfaithfulness of one's husband or wife in having sexual relations with another. According to this interpretation, scripture permits the remarriage only of the "innocent party." All other remarriage is forbidden as long as one's original mate is still living. All other remarriage is sin. Every one other than the innocent party who is married to another than his or her original mate is an adulterer or an adulteress.

It is necessary to emphasize this because there are many today—not only individuals but also churches—who appeal to Matthew 19:9 in support of remarriage, but who go far beyond what Matthew 19:9 teaches on even the most lenient interpretation of the text. They permit the remarriage not only of the innocent party, but also of the guilty party. They allow remarriage as well as divorce for every cause just as did the wicked Jews of Jesus' day. In practice and by official ecclesiastical decision, their answer to the question of the Pharisees, "Is it lawful for a man to put away his wife for every cause?" (vs. 3) is, "Yes; and having done so, you may with a free conscience marry another." The appeal of such people to Matthew 19:9 in support of remarriage is not made in good faith, for at the very most Matthew 19:9 permits the remarriage of the innocent party.

However, the text does not state that the innocent party may remarry. This is an inference that some draw from the text, but it is not Jesus' express statement. What Jesus says is that the man who divorces his wife for a reason other than fornication and then remarries, commits adultery. This is not to deny that the truth is sometimes implied in a text. But it is dangerous to base so weighty a doctrine as remarriage, and one so critically important for the practical life of God's people, on the shallow foundation of a mere implication. This is especially risky when the passage, the implication of which is supposed to bear all this weight, is not even mainly concerned with remarriage, but with divorce. This is positively wrong when the inference that is supposed to be drawn from the text contradicts the explicit testimony of scripture in other passages where the subject of the possibility of remarriage is on the foreground.

Scripture Interprets Scripture

Elsewhere, scripture teaches plainly that remarriage is absolutely and unconditionally forbidden as long as one's original husband or wife is still living, and that the man or woman who remarries while a former mate is still living is guilty of adultery, regardless

THE UNBREAKABLE MARRIAGE BOND

of the ground on which he divorced his original mate. This is the warning of Luke 16:18: "whosoever putteth away his wife, and marrieth another, committeth adultery: and whosoever marrieth her that is put away from her husband committeth adultery." Jesus here treats the issue of remarriage and forbids it unconditionally.

First Corinthians 7:39 teaches that a woman is bound to her husband as long as he lives and that one has the right to marry another only when the original mate dies: "The wife is bound by the law as long as her husband liveth; but if her husband be dead, she is at liberty to be married to whom she will; only in the Lord."

The apostle here consciously raises the question, under what circumstances may a man or a woman marry again? and his answer is, only under the one circumstance: that the original mate dies. The same clear instruction is given in Romans 7:2–3:

2. For the woman which hath an husband is bound by the law to her husband so long as he liveth; but if the husband be dead, she is loosed from the law of her husband.
3. So then if, while her husband liveth, she be married to another man, she shall be called an adulteress: but if her husband be dead, she is free from that law; so that she is no adulteress, though she be married to another man.

Marriage is a lifelong, indissoluble bond. Only the death of one's husband or wife gives one the freedom to marry another person. A woman who remarries while her husband is living is an adulteress.

Mark 10:11–12 express Jesus' absolute, unqualified condemnation of remarriage. The passage in which this text is found is parallel to Matthew 19. After the Lord has spoken to the Pharisees,

Jesus' disciples privately question him further about his strong statements to the Pharisees (v. 10). To the disciples Jesus says, "Whosoever shall put away his wife, and marry another, committeth adultery against her. And if a woman shall put away her husband, and be married to another, she committeth adultery."

It seems that in his remarks to his disciples Jesus concentrates more on the matter of remarriage, whereas with the Pharisees he had to do mainly with divorce. His position on remarriage is that remarriage is forbidden, without any qualification. If Matthew 19:9 implies the right of remarriage, it is the only passage in scripture to do so. One then faces the question of the harmony of this permission of remarriage with the other New Testament passages that clearly forbid all remarriage. But Matthew 19:9 does not imply the right of remarriage on the ground of the fornication of one's mate. That which might seem to indicate that the text is giving a ground for remarriage is the phrase "except it be for fornication." But the question is, what in the text do these words go with and qualify? Do they qualify "put away" or "marry another"? Does this phrase give a ground for divorce, or does it give a ground also for remarrying?

In answering the question we must remember that the subject is *divorce.* The Pharisees had asked about the legitimacy of divorce (v. 3). Jesus strictly forbade divorce (v. 6). The Pharisees had appealed to Moses' tolerance of divorce (v. 7) and pressed him further on the matter of divorce. In his final word to the Pharisees, of which verse 9 is part, Jesus is still concerned with divorce, as verse 8 shows: "Moses...suffered you to put away your wives: but from the beginning it was not so." Therefore, when Jesus states "except it be for fornication," he gives the one lawful ground for divorce and not a ground for remarriage.

Why then does he immediately mention remarriage and the

wickedness of remarriage, namely, adultery? Simply because he well knew the reason men usually put away their wives and the evil that generally follows divorce, namely, the evil of marrying another.

The first part of the text says nothing about the lawfulness or unlawfulness of the remarriage of the man whose wife has been guilty of fornication. It only states that divorce on any ground except fornication is forbidden and that the remarriage that follows such a divorce is sinful. It is understandable that the question arises: What then about the man whose wife has been unfaithful to him, whose wife has played the harlot with another man? He may divorce her, but may he marry another? The answer cannot be determined from the first part of the text. We must look elsewhere in scripture.

The Innocent Party May Not Remarry

We must first look at what Jesus says in the second part of Matthew 19:9: "And whoso marrieth her which is put away doth commit adultery." Here the Lord treats the remarriage of the woman who has been divorced by her husband, although she was not guilty of fornication. According to the first part of the text, she has been put away unjustly. In addition her husband has married another; he has made himself guilty of adultery. The poor woman is the innocent party. Now, what about her? May she marry another? If the view of those who hold that the innocent party may remarry is correct, the answer must be an emphatic yes. She is an innocent party. Her husband has committed adultery. No reconciliation is possible anymore, for her husband is married to another woman. But the answer of Jesus is, "Whoso marrieth her which is put away doth commit adultery." The innocent party may not remarry. Jesus' teaching on remarriage, therefore, is in perfect harmony with his doctrine, and the apostles' doctrine elsewhere in the New Testament. Although divorce is permitted on the one ground of fornication, remarriage is always prohibited, as long as one's mate is living.

The reason for the prohibition of remarriage must be found in the very nature of marriage as a divine institution. Marriage is a bond between two people that God establishes. Marriage is a bond that only God can and may dissolve. Only God dissolves the one flesh so that the two are no longer one, but two, and he does this through death. Death dissolves all the earthly ties, including marriage. In the very nature of it, marriage is for life. By its very nature, marriage cannot and may not be dissolved by man. "What therefore God hath joined together, let not man put asunder" (Matt. 19:6).

Even adultery does not dissolve the marriage bond. Adultery is a horrible laceration of the one flesh. It can so mutilate the marriage bond that the two have to live separately. But even in such a case, the attack on marriage is an action of man that does not break the bond so as to make another marriage possible. Still the wife is bound to her husband as long as he lives.

This is the profoundest meaning of Jesus' answer in verses 5–6 to the Pharisees' question about divorce. Theirs was a frivolous conception of marriage, for they viewed it as a bond that man could break. Their only question was whether man could break it for lighter or weightier causes. Jesus had a radically different view of marriage, as his answer showed. For his answer was, no divorce!

No divorce in the sense of a human dissolution of the marriage bond. The reason is that God has made two people into one flesh! And one flesh they will remain until God comes to put asunder.

Costly Discipleship

The Lord's prohibition of remarriage means the possibility of hardship for a believer. Jesus' disciples immediately saw this implication of his "hard sayings" on marriage and raised the objection of the practical difficulties that men were exposed to by his doctrine. "If the case of the man be so with his wife, it is not good to marry" (Matt. 19:10). One may have to suffer lifelong loneliness. A man's wife may leave him for another man, and he must remain unmarried as long as she lives. Christ speaks of this in verse 12: "there be eunuchs, which have made themselves eunuchs for the kingdom of heaven's sake." Or as Paul mentions in 1 Corinthians 7:11, a woman may have to leave her husband and remain single all the rest of her life.

Much of the disobedience of the churches today to the word of Christ on marriage, divorce, and remarriage is due to their refusal to permit such hardships among their people. The churches are busy avoiding the sufferings that belong to discipleship of Christ. They make the life of the Christian easy, not only in marriage but also in the other areas. They see the affliction of the people in their admittedly painful circumstances, and they say, "Jesus would never want anyone to have such a hard life." Then they quickly change Jesus' word so that he says what they think he should say. This is a temptation also for us.

But discipleship is costly. Never may the church preach any other message. Would you follow Christ? Then deny yourself. Take up your cross. Will to lose your life. Hate your father and mother, wife and children, brothers and sisters, yes, and your own very dear life.

Be prepared to be a eunuch for the kingdom's sake, if this should be required of you. Count the cost before you begin to follow Jesus.

This does not suggest that Jesus is not a sympathetic, compassionate savior. We have a high priest who can be touched with the feeling of our infirmities, so that we can come boldly to his throne of grace to obtain mercy and find grace to help in time of need (Heb. 4:15–16). No matter how difficult and painful the way of a disciple of Christ may be with regard to marriage, Christ will give him the grace obediently and patiently to walk on that way. Of course, it would be impossible for him to endure such a life in his own strength. But he looks to Christ for his strength. In response to the disciples' objection that his teaching on marriage opens the way to hardships, Jesus pointed to the sufficiency of his grace. He said, "All men cannot receive this saying, save they to whom it is given" (Matt. 19:11). And he declared that, by virtue of his grace, "there be eunuchs, which have made themselves eunuchs for the kingdom of heaven's sake" (v. 12).

In addition Jesus promises an abundant reward to those who suffer loss for his sake, including loss in marital life. At the end of Matthew 19, he says, "And every one that hath forsaken houses, or brethren, or sisters, or father, or mother, or wife, or children, or lands, for my name's sake, shall receive an hundredfold, and shall inherit everlasting life" (v. 29).

Privileged with a High Calling

We must not misunderstand Jesus' doctrine of marriage. The rigorous prohibition of divorce and remarriage is not intended to oppress and grieve the church. Rather, the purpose is to impress on the saints their lofty calling in marriage and thus to bless their marriages and homes.

We are called to reflect the covenant relationship between Jesus and his church in our marriages. Marriage is the mystery of Christ and the church. God instituted marriage as a symbol of the eternal covenant of grace between himself in Jesus Christ and his elect church. The covenant is intimate fellowship: Christ and the church become one flesh. By the grace of God, the covenant is unbreakable. Christ is faithful to his bride. He never puts her away and marries another. This is our salvation and our comfort. We have an eternal covenant of grace with God. We belong to our faithful savior Jesus Christ, in life and death, in time and eternity. By the power of the love and grace of Jesus Christ, the church on her part is faithful to him. She never forsakes him for another. On earth she cleaves to him and reverences him as he is revealed in his word.

Throughout her history she lives in the one hope of the coming of her bridegroom, her perfect union with him then, and the everlasting marriage. "Come, Lord Jesus" (Rev. 22:20).

Our calling in marriage is to reflect this unbreakable covenant. What a difference this makes practically. The young people of the church, knowing marriage as a lifelong bond, regard marriage with the seriousness it demands. It is not a casual arrangement, easily made and as easily broken. They will take care whom they marry and how they marry. They will marry "only in the Lord" (1 Cor. 7:39). The married saints will be faithful. The prohibition of remarriage, the exclusion of a third party, is to us only an underscoring of our positive calling: be faithful to your own wife or your own husband.

If every new relationship is forbidden, it follows that I ought to set myself to the work of maintaining and deepening and enriching the relationship God has given me.

Exactly in this way, the result of Jesus' teaching on marriage will be strong and happy marriages in the church. This is bliss! Where there are strong and happy marriages, there will also be solid homes and rich family life. This is delightful! These are the joys Christ aimed at for his people when he taught us about marriage.

Jesus' doctrine of marriage comforts us. Our desire is that our marriages be maintained, although they are always threatened by our weakness and sin. Now we hear from the mouth of the Lord himself that God maintains the marriage bond and that he has a special concern for its maintenance. Certainly he will help us when we pray to him on behalf of our marriages, for his own glory is involved in our marriages.

Scripture's teaching on marriage puts us before the face of God as we live in marriage. Ultimately, we do not stand before our wife or husband, before our children, before the church, or before society. We stand in the presence of the Most High and ever blessed God. Carrying out our calling with regard to marriage, we have to do with our heavenly Father.

Whatever this may mean for you personally, stand before his face daily. Thus expect soon the real marriage, before whose unutterably glorious reality the earthly picture fades away: the marriage of the Lamb and his wife, the church, who "hath made herself ready" (Rev. 19:7).

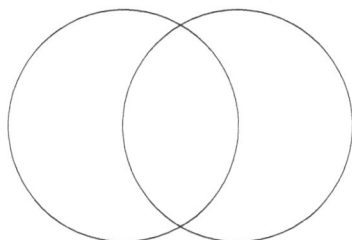

Section Two

A BRIEF HISTORY OF THE CHURCH'S DOCTRINE OF MARRIAGE

10

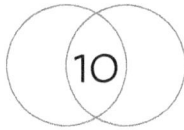

The Development
of Herman Hoeksema

In the first section of this book, I contend for a doctrine of marriage that views marriage as a lifelong bond established by God. Only God may and only God can dissolve the bond that he has created. This implies that divorce in the sense of the breaking of the bond is not only impermissible but also impossible for man. The divorce that scripture allows in Matthew 5:31–32 and in Matthew 19:9 is a legal separation of bed and board, not a dissolving of the bond. Such a separation is permitted only in the case of fornication, that is, the sexual infidelity of one's wife or husband. Even in the case of divorce on the ground of fornication, the bond made by God at the marriage of the two is not broken. The "innocent party" in the divorce, therefore, is not permitted by God to many another. If the innocent party does remarry, his new relationship is an adulterous marriage.

According to the institution of marriage in Genesis 2:18–25, God's act of marriage makes one flesh of the two persons and binds them for life. The nature of marriage, therefore, forbids all remarriage after divorce. Liberty to marry again comes only by the death of one's marriage companion. The apostle wrote in

1 Corinthians 7:39, "The wife is bound by the law as long as her husband liveth; but if her husband be dead, she is at liberty to be married to whom she will; only in the Lord."

This doctrine of marriage is not only my personal conviction, but it is also the teaching of a denomination of Reformed churches. For the past half-century and more the Protestant Reformed Churches in America have taught and practiced this doctrine of marriage with its implications for divorce and remarriage. This doctrine of marriage is church doctrine.

The Protestant Reformed Churches were led to this understanding of the biblical doctrine of marriage by Reformed theologian Herman Hoeksema. In a series of editorials entitled "Unbiblical Divorce and Remarriage" in the periodical the *Standard Bearer* in 1956–57, Hoeksema "showed from the word of God that the marriage tie can never be broken except by death."[1]

In a pamphlet published about the same time as the articles in the *Standard Bearer,* Hoeksema forcefully asserted his stand on marriage, divorce, and remarriage:

My stand is that the marriage bond is absolutely unbreakable for life. My stand is that a man may certainly put away his wife if that becomes absolutely necessary, but she is still his wife, even after she is divorced. And my stand is that therefore when anyone marries that woman that is divorced, divorced even on Biblical grounds, say,

---

1 Herman Hoeksema, "Unbiblical Divorce and Remarriage," *Standard Bearer* 33, no. 8 (January 15, 1957): 172. This was the concluding installment of the series. Previous articles appeared in the issues of September 15, 1956: 485–87; October 1, 1956: 5–6; October 15, 1956: 29–30; November 1, 1956: 52–53; November 15, 1956: 76; December 1, 1956: 100; December 15, 1956: 125; and January 1, 1957: 148–49. These articles were published as a booklet titled *Unbiblical Divorce and Remarriage* (Grand Rapids, MI: Reformed Free Publishing Association, n.d.).

that man also commits the sin of adultery...Why?

Because the marriage relation before God is absolutely unbreakable until death.[2]

In this pamphlet, as in the series of editorials in the *Standard Bearer*, Hoeksema grounded this stand, first, in the unbreakable covenant of grace between God and his people in Christ. An unbreakable bond of marriage follows from the unbreakable covenant because marriage is the earthly picture of the covenant: "Principally the marriage relation is unbreakable, because it rests in the reflection of God's unbreakable covenant."[3]

Second, the basis was the teaching of the New Testament on marriage, divorce, and remarriage. Hoeksema pointed to Matthew 19:9; Mark 10:11–12; Luke 16:18; and 1 Corinthians 7:39. The second part of Matthew 19:9 was decisive for Hoeksema on the question whether the innocent party may remarry. Christ's word is "and whoso marrieth her which is put away doth commit adultery." By this word the Lord forbids the remarriage of the woman whose husband has unjustly divorced her and has then sinfully married another woman.

This settles the matter conclusively. Notice that there are three parties here, or really four parties; but that second wife is not taken into consideration. There is the first husband that puts away his wife. She didn't commit adultery. She was entirely innocent. She never violated the marriage bond by committing adultery. Nevertheless, he put away his wife. Secondly, he remarries, marries another woman.

---

2 Herman Hoeksema, *The Unbreakable Bond of Marriage* (Grand Rapids, MI: Sunday School Mission Publishing Society, n.d.; repr. 1969), 17.

3 Ibid., 10.

Now the second party enters in—another man. Notice: the man put away his wife and married another woman. May that first woman now enter into a marriage relationship with another man? On the contrary, for the Lord says: "And whoso marrieth her which is put away doth commit adultery." That second party therefore, may not marry the innocent woman. To marry her is also adultery. And why is that so? Why is this marrying with the innocent woman called adultery? Simply because she is still married to the first man, although he had already married another woman. This, therefore, is the plain truth of Scripture.[4]

Hoeksema's Earliest View

Hoeksema freely acknowledged that this stand represented a change in his thinking. Earlier in his ministry he had uncritically accepted and advocated the view that once generally prevailed in the Reformed tradition. This was the view that the adultery of one's marriage companion not only allowed one to divorce the sinning wife or husband but also to remarry. This view was popularly known as the right of the remarriage of the innocent party.

I must confess that without considering the matter very thoroughly I used to agree with the old stand of the Christian Reformed Church, namely, that when a man committed adultery, the woman may not only divorce him, but may also remarry. At that time I did not confront the question very definitely, and did not consider it very deeply...After considering the whole matter in the light of Scripture, however, I must now radically

---

4 Ibid., 16.

oppose this position. And against this stand I now take the position that marriage is forever unbreakable, is always for life, no matter what happens.[5]

In 1933 Hoeksema had publicly voiced the view that he would later renounce. He did this in two articles in the *Standard Bearer* in response to a question concerning the meaning of Matthew 19:9.[6] In these articles Hoeksema maintained, first, that 1 Corinthians 7:39 does not teach that *only* death dissolves a marriage; second, that the exception clause in Matthew 19:9 means that "if someone divorces his wife on account of fornication and marries another he does not commit adultery. The innocent party, therefore, in such a case has the right to divorce and also to proceed with a new marriage"; and, third, that the exception clause in Matthew 19:9 cannot be explained as applying only to the prohibition against divorce. It applies also to the phrase regarding remarriage. Fourth, Hoeksema maintained that "scripture indeed views fornication as the dissolving [*vernietiging*] of the bond of marriage." Significantly, even then Hoeksema was convinced that the second part of Matthew 19:9 prohibits the remarriage of the innocent wife whose husband has unjustly divorced her and married another woman. In 1933 Hoeksema took the position that the sexual unfaithfulness of one's wife or husband within marriage (that is, fornication) dissolved the marriage and gave to the innocent party the right to remarry. But he denied that an unjust

---

5 Ibid., 12–13; see Hoeksema, *Unbiblical Divorce*, 20–21.

6 The question and the first installment of Hoeksema's answer appear under the title "*Vragen*" [Question] in the *Standard Bearer* 9, no. 16 (June 1, 1933): 374–77. The second installment of Hoeksema's answer, "*Antwoord Op de Vraag van Hudsonville*" [Answer to the question of Hudsonville] appears in the *Standard Bearer* 9, no. 18 (July 1, 1933): 424–26. The quotations from these articles are my translation of the Dutch.

divorce and the subsequent remarriage on the part of the divorced husband or wife (that is, adultery) gave the unjustly divorced wife or husband the right to remarry. He denied this on the basis of the second part of Matthew 19:9.

> Not adultery but fornication is named in the text as a possible ground for divorce. We come, therefore, to this conclusion, that, if there is no fornication, husband and wife are bound to each other and commit adultery if the one divorces the other, that is, the one who divorces commits adultery and the one who is divorced also always commits adultery if she (or he) remarries. Even though a divorced woman, who has been divorced by her husband without any basis of fornication, is innocent, she can never again marry. If she does marry, she commits adultery. The scripture views her as bound to the first husband. His adultery does not free her.[7]

Hoeksema's View in 1943

Careful study of scripture compelled Hoeksema to reject the position that he first adopted, namely, that the marriage bond is breakable in one instance; that fornication breaks the bond; and that the innocent party whose marriage companion has committed fornication may remarry.

Reconsideration of the traditional Reformed doctrine of marriage, divorce, and remarriage did not take place overnight. Although Hoeksema publicly renounced this tradition and recanted his earlier espousal of it in the middle 1950s, he had been rethinking his position for some time. This is evident from the

---

7 Hoeksema, "*Antwoord op de Vraag van Hudsonville*," 425–26.

editorial that he wrote in 1943 in answer to the question whether a confessing "member of a sound Reformed church may remarry, if he or she is divorced on biblical grounds." Whereas in 1933 Hoeksema had answered this question in the affirmative, now his mind had changed:

> I must confess that I myself have gradually undergone a change of conviction on this point in the course of the years by investigation of holy scripture. Earlier, without making much personal study of the question, I shared the most common opinion that the innocent party in a divorce may also marry again. I mean that this is the standpoint that is taken by most. It rests on the presupposition that divorce completely breaks the bond of marriage, so that the married parties are free from each other and, therefore, have also the right to proceed with another marriage...But I no longer share that opinion. I am increasingly confirmed in the conviction that fornication does indeed give to the innocent party in the marriage the right to divorce the guilty party (although this does not have to take place and forgiveness and reconciliation are indeed the requirement first of all), but that by this the bond of marriage is not broken as long as both parties live. And if this is the case, it lies in the nature of the case that neither of the divorced parties may remarry another.[8]

Already in 1943 Hoeksema's grounds for this position were

---

8 Herman Hoeksema, *"Hertrouwen van Gescheidenen"* [Remarriage of divorced (persons)], *Standard Bearer* 19, no. 16 (May 15, 1943): 364–65. The quotations from this article are my translation of the Dutch.

those that he would put forward in his more decisive break with the tradition in 1956–57.

> First…I think that in general scripture represents marriage as a reflection of God's covenant with his people that he never breaks. That people can sin in that covenant and thus commit spiritual fornication, but the covenant lies absolutely firm in God, and he never gives his people a certificate of divorce.[9]

The second ground for his rejection in 1943 of the notion that fornication dissolves the bond of marriage so that the innocent party is permitted to remarry was the testimony of the New Testament passages that address this issue. Hoeksema mentioned Matthew 5:32; 19:9; Mark 10:11–12; and Luke 16:18. Taken together these passages are emphatic condemnation of all remarriage after divorce. With regard to the exception clause in Matthew 19:9, Hoeksema explained that it gives a ground only for divorce. It does not provide a ground for remarriage. Conclusive for the correct interpretation of the exception clause is the second part of Matthew 19:9. Even though the divorced woman is the innocent party in the divorce and even though her husband has contracted an adulterous marriage with another woman, this innocent party is forbidden by Christ to remarry.

> If anyone ever can have the right to remarry, it is certainly this woman. Her husband has, as much as lies in his power, totally broken the bond of marriage with his first wife by living in adultery. And still this woman does not have the

---

9   Ibid., 365.

right to remarry. On the contrary, whoever marries her, even after her husband has entered another marriage, is said to commit adultery. Why? There can only be one answer to this question: despite the sin of the husband, and despite her having been divorced, this woman is yet always bound before God to the living husband.[10]

Already in 1943 Hoeksema was firmly convinced that all remarriage is forbidden during the life of two married persons. The reason is that marriage is a bond that is broken only by death:

Therefore my answer is that there are indeed biblical grounds for divorce before the law so that husband and wife live in separation from each other. But this can never be viewed as such a breaking of the bond of marriage that either of the parties, guilty or innocent, can have the right to remarry until death separates them.[11]

It is worthy of note that Hoeksema, ever his own man when he was convinced that scripture constrained him, came to this stand in spite of the opposition, not only of the Reformed tradition but also of his own consistory. In the article in the May 15, 1943, issue of the *Standard Bearer* in which he expressed his conviction that the innocent party is not permitted to remarry after divorce, Hoeksema mentioned the disagreement of his consistory. Having referred to the viewpoint that the innocent party may remarry as the "most common opinion," Hoeksema continued, "this is also the point of view that is adopted again and again by the majority of my own consistory and, therefore, by my consistory as often

---

10 Ibid., 366.
11 Ibid.

as a concrete case comes up in our congregation today." He then added, "But I no longer share that opinion."[12]

It is also worthy of note that Hoeksema resolutely maintained his position publicly in the face of opposition from a prominent member of his own congregation. Hoeksema's editorial on the impermissibility of the remarriage of the innocent party drew a response from a member of his own congregation objecting to this position. This response resulted in a series of exchanges on the issue between the member and Hoeksema that were published in the *Standard Bearer*. The debate centered on the interpretation of Matthew 19:9, particularly the exception clause, "except it be for fornication."

Jesus' prohibition against the remarriage of the divorced woman in the second part of the text was decisive for Hoeksema. The fundamental importance of this second part of the one text that might be understood as allowing the remarriage of the innocent party for the correct interpretation, Hoeksema indicated by the titles he gave to the exchange: "And [What about] That Deserted [or Divorced, Woman] Then?"; "Once More: And [What about] the Deserted [Woman] Then?"; "Yet Once Again: [What about] That Deserted [Woman]?"[13]

Fully Developed View

Hoeksema set forth his doctrine of marriage, divorce, and remarriage in its fully developed form in his commentary on the Heidelberg Catechism. Explaining the Catechism's exposition in

---

12 Ibid., 364.

13 Herman Hoeksema, *"En Die Verlatene Dan?"* [And (what about) that deserted (woman) then?] *Standard Bearer* 20, no. 3 (November 1, 1943): 50–51; *"Nog Eens: En De Verlatene Dan?"* [Once more: And [what about] the deserted (woman) then?] *Standard Bearer* 20, no. 4 (November 15, 1943): 74–75; *"Nog Eenmaal: DIE Verlatene?"* [Yet once again: (What about) that deserted (woman)?] *Standard Bearer* 20, no. 5 (December 1, 1943): 96–98.

Lord's Day 41 of the seventh commandment of God's law, Hoeksema treated specifically the truth of marriage in two chapters, "The Covenant of Marriage" and "Divorce and Remarriage,"

He defined marriage as

> the union between one man and one woman for life, a union that is based on a communion of nature, on a communion of life, and a communion of love, which is a reflection of the covenant relation between God and His people and of the relation between Christ and His church; a union, moreover, that has its chief purpose in bringing forth the seed of the covenant.[14]

He asserted in the strongest language that every marriage is indissoluble:

> The marriage bond is absolutely indissoluble. It cannot be broken. No more than the union between Christ and His church can be dissolved, no more can the marriage tie ever be severed. It is a most intimate union of life and for life, which only death can dissolve.[15]

Hoeksema denied that the divorce permitted by scripture in Matthew 5:32 and 19:9 is the actual dissolution of the bond before the face of God so that the divorced persons are permitted to remarry. He defined biblical divorce thus: "Biblical divorce I

---

14 Herman Hoeksema, "The Covenant of Marriage," in *The Triple Knowledge: An Exposition of the Heidelberg Catechism* (Grand Rapids, MI: Reformed Free Publishing Association, 1972), 3:353.

15 Ibid., 3:354.

would define as a separation for life of married people, that is, a legal separation for life, on the basis of adultery or fornication."[16]

He called attention to the fact that this definition of divorce is fundamentally different from the definition that permits one or the other or both of the divorced persons to remarry:

> I put it this way intentionally, in distinction from others, who claim that a divorce is the dissolution of the marriage tie, so that after the dissolution the bond does no longer exist and the married people are and are permitted to act as if they were never married...It is my conviction that according to the Word of God, divorce can never mean dissolution of the marriage tie.
>
> Even if people are legally divorced, they are in my opinion according to the Word of God still married. Only, they are separate married people.[17]

Hoeksema did not hesitate explicitly to draw the conclusion concerning remarriage:

> The Bible teaches without any doubt that the marriage bond is indissoluble, that it can only be dissolved in death, and that therefore remarriage while both parties are still living is condemned by the Word of God.[18]

Hoeksema published this doctrine of marriage in his commentary on the Catechism, knowing full well that it would circulate widely in the Reformed world, at the exact time (1955)

---

16 Herman Hoeksema, "Divorce and Remarriage," in ibid., 3:359.
17 Ibid.
18 Ibid., 3:367.

when Reformed churches were beginning to relax their marriage doctrine under the pressures of the adulterous world in which the churches were living. What Hoeksema observed concerning the laws of the land at that time was beginning to be true also of the laws of the churches: "The laws of our land have fast retreated before the wild rush of the carnal lust of the nation, until they are no longer a protection of the sacred bond of matrimony.[19]

Convinced by this great theologian that the word of God does indeed teach marriage as a lifelong, unbreakable bond in reflection of the everlasting covenant of grace, the Protestant Reformed Churches have steadfastly confessed and practiced this doctrine of marriage with its implications for divorce and remarriage to the present day.

This doctrine of marriage has been a mighty instrument for the preservation of marriages and for the blessing of families in these churches. It has enabled them to bear witness against the appalling, scandalous disobedience to the will of God concerning marriage in the evangelical and Reformed churches today. In addition the unbreakable bond of marriage is an important aspect of the great gospel truth of the faithful, unbreakable covenant of grace between God and his elect church in Jesus Christ, the real marriage of which earthly marriage is a symbol.

---

19 Ibid., 3:357. The book in which Hoeksema's doctrine of marriage first appeared was published as Herman Hoeksema, *Love Thy Neighbor for God's Sake*, vol. 9, *The Triple Knowledge: The Heidelberg Catechism, An Exposition, Part Three: Of Thankfulness* (Grand Rapids, MI: Wm. B. Eerdmans Publishing Co., 1955), 83–107.

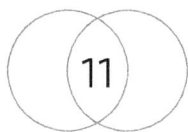

11

The Reformed Tradition

The doctrine of marriage as an unbreakable bond until death represents a break with the Reformed tradition. Originating in the Reformation of the sixteenth century with the reformers themselves, the Reformed tradition has held that, although marriage is ideally a lifelong bond by virtue of God's institution and intention, the marriage relationship can be dissolved by sinful human behavior. One sinful act that breaks the relationship is the sexual infidelity of the husband or the wife. Fornication in Matthew 5:31–32 and in Matthew 19:9 is the adultery of one of the married persons, and adultery dissolves, or can possibly dissolve, the marriage so as to permit the innocent party to remarry. In the main the Reformed tradition has until very recently been adamant that adultery permits only the innocent party to remarry. The guilty party has been forbidden to remarry.

The other sinful act that has been recognized in the Reformed tradition as dissolving a marriage is the desertion of a believer by an unbelieving husband or wife. Advocacy of desertion as a valid ground of both divorce and remarriage is based on a specific understanding of Paul's teaching in 1 Corinthians 7:15: "But if the unbelieving depart, let him depart. A brother or a sister is not under bondage in such cases: but God hath called us to peace." This understanding supposes that the apostle teaches that the abandoned believer is no longer "bound" to the deserter, as though "not under bondage" is the same as "is not bound."

The words that follow, "but God hath called us to peace," are explained as meaning that God gives the abandoned believer the right to remarry. Desertion as a ground of remarriage is known as the "Pauline privilege," since it is thought to be Paul's adding of a ground for divorce and remarriage to the ground given by Christ in Matthew 19:9, namely, adultery.

The Dutch Reformed

Not all Reformed churches and theologians, however, have agreed that desertion constitutes a biblical ground for remarriage. Prior to 1956 the Christian Reformed Church for many years took a firm stand that only adultery breaks the marriage tie and that in this case only the innocent party may remarry. Describing the stand of the Christian Reformed Church before 1956, J. L. Schaver wrote, "Adultery is the only biblical ground for divorce...Willful separation is not considered a biblical ground for divorce.[1]

The "Report of the Committee on 'Marital Problems'" to the Reformed Ecumenical Synod of Edinburgh 1953 addressed the matter of biblical grounds for divorce:

---

1 J. L. Schaver, *The Polity of the Churches*, 4th rev. ed. (Grand Rapids, MI: International Publications, 1956), 2:225. Schaver gives the gist of certain ecclesiastical cases involving complicated marital situations that make plain that the Christian Reformed Church was long determined to condemn and keep out of the church all remarriages except those of the innocent party. Particular decisions of the Christian Reformed Synod of 1936 were inconsistent according to Schaver (2:225–32).

The case of adultery is quite clear. In the case of 1 Cor. 7:15 (desertion because of religious hatred), it can be a matter of opinion if divorce with the right to remarry should be granted or only separation of bed and board.[2]

The Reformed Ecumenical Synod of Potchefstroom, South Africa, adopted the recommendation of its committee rejecting the view that 1 Corinthians 7:15 provides a ground for divorce and subsequent remarriage:

> As regards so-called malicious desertion, it appears to us that, as declared by the American report in the Agenda, we have to do in 1 Corinthians 7:15 with a very special case. Here we have a desertion *religionis causa* [on account of religion]. We must pay attention here to the context of the whole chapter which possesses par excellence a pastoral character. Paul, as Apostle, here supplies incidental advice for specific situations facing believers in his times. To believers as a result of the commandment of Christ he expressly disallows the dissolution of a marriage and contraction of a second (1 Corinthians 7:10–11). In addition he distinguishes another type of marriage, viz. that between a believer and an unbeliever. It appears to us that we have to do here with marriages of heathen, one of whom then became a believer. The question then arose in the case of desertion of the unbelieving partner whether the believing partner should keep insisting on the restitution of the

---

2 "Report of the Committee on 'Marital Problems,'" in *Acts of the Reformed Ecumenical Synod Edinburgh 1953* (Edinburgh: Lindsay & Co. Ltd., 1953), 91. Even though its recognition of adultery as a ground of divorce refers to a right of the innocent party to remarry, the report immediately adds: "The *conclusion* of your committee is that marriage as a divine ordinance has in its essence the character of a lifelong union" (91–92).

marriage. It has been accepted by some that Paul's answer to the question has the nature of a so-called second ground for divorce. In the opinion of your commission this is certainly not the case. It is especially in this case incorrect to speak of a "Scriptural ground for divorce." Judging from the context the following appears to be the case: The man had deserted the wife as a result of religious friction or hatred, and Paul felt that for the Christian wife it was necessary to accept the situation. The question of how far Paul implied by the expression of 7:15 ("A brother or a sister is not under bondage in such cases") that the marriage is here legally dissolved, cannot be answered on exegetical grounds. It is also not clear here whether he allowed a second marriage in such cases.[3]

Indicative of the reluctance, particularly within the Dutch Reformed tradition, to recognize desertion as a ground of divorce and remarriage on the basis of 1 Corinthians 7:15 is the commentary of the highly respected exegete F. W. Grosheide. Commenting on Matthew 19:9, Grosheide freely states:

There is but one cause why divorce may follow, namely, fornication, that is, the actual dissolving of the marriage... Jesus calls this the only reason (*er maar een oorzaak is, waarop echtscheiding volgen mag, n. l. hoererij, dat is de feitelijke verbreking van het huwelijk...Jezus noemt dit de eenige reden*).[4]

---

3 *Acts of the Fourth Reformed Ecumenical Synod of Potchefstroom, South Africa 1958* (Potchefstroom: Potchefstroom Herald, 1958), 98.

4 F. W. Grosheide, *Het Heilig Evangelie volgens Mattheus* [The holy gospel according to Matthew] (Amsterdam: H. A. van Bottenburp, 1922), 226. The translation of the Dutch is mine.

In his commentary on 1 Corinthians 7:15, Grosheide says not one word about any breaking of the bond by the unbeliever's desertion of the believer. Nor does he so much as hint that the deserted believer might have a right to remarry. That the deserted believer is "not under bondage" means that he or she does not have to try at all cost to prevent the unbeliever from leaving. The "peace" of the deserted believer is the peace with God and with the neighbor that would be disturbed if the believer continually would have to restrain the unbeliever from separating.[5]

Nevertheless, H. Bouwman presents the marriage doctrine of the Reformed Churches in the Netherlands as approving remarriage on the grounds both of adultery and of desertion. Bouwman does admit that it is not "decisively expressed" in 1 Corinthians 7:15 whether "the Christian party who is left alone may indeed marry again...or must remain unmarried." But Bouwman is confident that "the marriage bond is broken by that deliberate desertion, and the deserted party can again make a new marriage." The position that adultery and malicious desertion are lawful grounds of divorce and remarriage, says Bouwman, has been the position of the Reformed theologians in the Netherlands almost without exception. He mentions Danaeus, Junius, Ames, Rivet, Van Mastricht, and à Brakel as taking this position.[6]

In harmony with Bouwman's analysis of the Dutch Reformed tradition as permitting divorce and remarriage on the two grounds of adultery and desertion is the position of Dutch Reformed ethicist W. Geesink. In his explanation of the seventh commandment,

---

5 F. W. Grosheide, *Commentary on the First Epistle to the Corinthians* (Grand Rapids, MI: Wm. B. Eerdmans Publishing Co., 1974), 166–67.

6 H. Bouwman, "*Echtscheiding*," in *Christelijke Encyclopaedie voor het Nederlandsche Volk* ["Divorce," in Christian encyclopedia for the Dutch people], ed. F. W. Grosheide, J. H. Landwehr, C. Lindeboom, J. C. Rullmann (Kampen: J. H. Kok, n.d.), 2:3–13. The translation of the Dutch is mine.

Geesink states that, according to the word of God, the magistrate may grant a divorce only on the grounds of adultery and malicious desertion. By divorce Geesink understands the dissolution of the marriage. Significantly, Geesink observes that the granting of the divorce by the magistrate is merely the declaration that a marriage that has already been dissolved, presumably by the sinful act of adultery or desertion, is indeed dissolved.[7]

The notes in the margin of the Dutch *Staten Bijbel* explain 1 Corinthians 7:15 as permitting the deserted believer to remarry: "that is, not required from their side to maintain the bond of marriage any longer or to remain unmarried" (my translation of the Dutch).

The Presbyterians

The Presbyterian wing of the Reformed tradition likewise has viewed marriage as a relationship that can be dissolved both by adultery and by desertion so that both the innocent party and the deserted believer are allowed to remarry.

John Murray explained Matthew 19:9 as the Lord's teaching that

> when a man puts away his wife for the cause of fornication this putting away has the effect of dissolving the bond of marriage with the result that he is free to remarry without thereby incurring the guilt of adultery. In simple terms it means that divorce in such a case dissolves the marriage and that the parties are no longer man and wife.[8]

---

7   W. Geesink, *Van's Heeren Ordinantien* [Concerning the Lord's ordinances] (Kampen: J. H. Kok, 1925), 4:226.

8   John Murray, *Divorce* (Philadelphia: Presbyterian and Reformed, 1961), 43.

Although Murray concluded that 1 Corinthians 7:15 does permit a believer deserted by an unbelieving marriage companion to remarry, he was very cautious, even tentative, in reaching and teaching this conclusion. Murray called the explanation of the verb translated by the King James Version as "is not under bondage" in 1 Corinthians 7:15 "one of the most perplexing questions in New Testament interpretation." He recognized that the Greek word does not obviously refer to dissolution of the marriage bond. In addition, to explain the word as giving a ground for divorce and remarriage would seemingly bring Paul into conflict with Christ. In the view of those who explain Matthew 19:9 as offering a biblical ground for remarriage after divorce, Christ gave one, and one only, ground for remarriage: the fornication of one's wife or husband. Paul, in defiance of Christ, adds yet another ground. These considerations led Murray frankly to acknowledge that "it is difficult to make out a strong or valid case for the view that *ou dedoulootai* (is not under bondage) means dissolution."

Nevertheless, Murray found "cogent arguments" also on the other side of the question and came to the conclusion that "there is much to be said in favour of the view that 1 Corinthians 7:15 contemplates the dissolution of the bond of marriage."[9]

However, immediately upon concluding that 1 Corinthians 7:15 permits a believer deserted by an unbeliever to remarry, Murray deplored the abuse of the "Pauline privilege" by Presbyterians. The abuse is that those in the church who have been abandoned—not by an unbeliever for religious reasons, but by professing Christians for other reasons—appeal to the "privilege" in support of their actions of divorcing and remarrying.

In this connection Murray was critical of the Westminster

---

9 Ibid., 69–78.

Confession's treatment of "wilful desertion" as a ground of divorce and remarriage in chapter 24.6. The Confession failed "to confine the liberty of dissolution to the precise conditions prescribed by the apostle in this passage," leaving a "loophole...[that] cannot be maintained on the basis of Scripture."[10]

The significance of Murray's criticism should not be underestimated. He charges the Westminster divines with serious error in their understanding and application of 1 Corinthians 7:15.

If the text does provide another ground for divorce and remarriage besides adultery, as is Murray's tentative position, it provides this ground only to a believer who has been deserted by an unbeliever because the unbeliever hates Christ. It does not permit a professing Christian to remarry when his wife, who also professes Christianity, has left him because of his abuse of her. It does not permit a professing Christian to remarry when her husband, who also professes Christianity, has left her because both agree that they are not compatible and are not enjoying their life together. But the Westminster Confession allows for divorce and remarriage in such circumstances: "such wilful desertion as can no way be remedied by the church or civil magistrate." Presbyterians are availing themselves of this "loophole." The result is that Presbyterians are living in adultery with the approval, not only of their churches but also of the Westminster Confession of Faith.

The expression of the characteristic Presbyterian position on marriage, divorce, and remarriage by the Southern Presbyterian Robert L. Dabney is noteworthy for several things. It acknowledges that marriage is ideally dissolved only by death. It insists that adultery and desertion are the only two sins that "annihilate" the bond. It suggests that the reason a bond that is ideally lifelong can yet be

10 Ibid., 77–78.

dissolved while both marriage partners are living is that an adulterous or deserting marriage companion may be regarded as "dead."

> Under the New Testament, divorce proper can take place only on two grounds, adultery and permanent desertion. See Matt. 19:9, 5:32; 1 Cor. 7:15. A careful examination of these passages will lead us to these truths: That marriage is a permanent and exclusive union of one woman to one man; and so, can only be innocently dissolved by death: But that extreme criminality and breach of contract by one party annihilates the bond so that the criminal is as though he were dead to the other: That the only sins against the bond, which have this effect, are those which are absolutely incompatible with the relation, adultery, and wilful, final desertion. In these cases, the bond having been destroyed for the innocent party, he is as completely a single man, as though the other were dead. Some commonwealths have added many other trivial causes of divorce; thus sinning grievously against God and the purity of the people. The Church may not recognize by her officers or acts, any of these unscriptural grounds, or the pretended divorces founded on them.[11]

John Owen spoke for both the older Presbyterians and the Puritans.

> Adultery is a just and sufficient cause of a divorce... [which] consists in a dissolution *"vinculi matrimonialis* [of the bond of marriage]" and so removes the marriage

---

11 Robert L. Dabney, *Lectures in Systematic Theology* (Grand Rapids, MI: Zondervan Publishing House, repr. 1972), 409–10.

relation as that the innocent person divorcing or procuring the divorce is at liberty to marry again. [12]

As for the "Pauline privilege,"

the apostle Paul expressly sets the party at liberty to marry who is maliciously and obstinately deserted, affirming that the Christian religion doth not prejudice the natural right and privilege of men in such cases: 1 Cor. 7:15.[13]

Acceptance of adultery and desertion as grounds of lawful divorce and remarriage and, with this, the view of marriage as a contract that can be voided by the actions of men are creedal positions for Presbyterians. Whereas the distinctively Reformed creeds—the Heidelberg Catechism, the Belgic Confession, and the Canons of Dordt—do not pronounce on marriage, divorce, and remarriage, the Presbyterian Westminster Confession of Faith does. With appeal to Matthew 19:9, it approves the remarriage of the innocent party: "In the case of adultery after marriage, it is lawful for the innocent party to sue out a divorce, and, after the divorce, to marry another, as if the offending party were dead."[14]

On the basis of 1 Corinthians 7:15, the Westminster Confession also approves the remarriage of the deserted believer.

Although the corruption of man be such as is apt to study arguments, unduly to put asunder those whom God hath

---

12 John Owen, "Of Marrying after Divorce in Case of Adultery," in *The Works of John Owen*, ed. William H. Goold (London: Banner of Truth Trust, repr. 1968), 16:254.

13 Ibid., 16:257.

14 Westminster Confession of Faith 24.5, in *The Subordinate Standards and Other Authoritative Documents of the Free Church of Scotland* (Edinburgh: William Blackwood & Sons Ltd., 1973), 38.

joined together in marriage; yet nothing but adultery or such wilful desertion as can no way he remedied by the church or civil magistrate, is cause sufficient of dissolving the bond of marriage.[15]

In spite of the general agreement between the three forms of unity and the Westminster standards, so serious a matter is the Westminster Confession's approval of remarriage after divorce that this would stand in the way of full ecclesiastical relationships between a church that subscribed to the Westminster Confession and a denomination of churches that held in a heartfelt way the indissolubility of marriage. A divorced and remarried member of the former would not be accepted at the Lord's table in the latter.

A Presbyterian officebearer who was convinced of the impermissibility of remarriage after divorce would have to sign his subscription to the Westminster Confession with stated objection against its teaching on marriage, divorce, and remarriage in chapter 24.5–6.

Despite this confessional statement, there have been prominent Presbyterians who have questioned whether desertion dissolves a marriage and whether such a doctrine can be drawn from the apostle's teaching in 1 Corinthians 7:15. The Presbyterian theologian Robert Shaw acknowledged this in his commentary on the Westminster Confession:

There can be no question that adultery is a just ground for "the innocent party to sue out a divorce, and, after the divorce, to marry another, as if the offending party were dead"...But whether the wilful and obstinate desertion of

---

15 Westminster Confession of Faith 24.6, in ibid.

one of the parties sets the other party at liberty to marry again may admit of dispute.[16]

Shaw mentioned Dr. Dwight as one who opposed the interpretation of 1 Corinthians 7:15 that finds in the passage a dissolving of the marriage bond.

Shaw's defense of the Confession's doctrine concerning desertion is notable for its hesitancy:

> But at verse 15 [the apostle] *appears* to declare that the party who was deserted was free to marry again. And the decision *seems* just…it is not *reasonable* that the innocent party should be denied all relief.[17]

Shaw calls attention to an aspect of the issue that is often overlooked by those who contend that adultery and desertion are grounds for remarriage because they dissolve the marriage bond:

> Adultery does not, *ipso facto*, dissolve the bond of marriage, nor may it be dissolved by consent of parties. The violation of the marriage vow only invests the injured party with a right to demand the dissolution of it by the competent authority; and if he chooses to exercise that right, the divorce must be effected "by a public and orderly course of proceeding."[18]

Neither adultery nor desertion dissolves the marriage bond. The married parties themselves do not have the right to dissolve

---

16 Robert Shaw, *An Exposition of the Westminster Confession of Faith* (Inverness, Scotland: Christian Focus Publications, 1974), 257–58.

17 Ibid., 258; emphases added.

18 Ibid.

their marriage. Who or what, then, does have the right and the might to dissolve a marriage so that divorced persons may remarry? According to Robert Shaw, it is the state that dissolves the marriage bond at the demand of the injured party. What God has joined together, the state has authority and might to put asunder at the wish of the married persons.

The Reformers

The prevailing view in the Reformed tradition—that adultery certainly and desertion probably are valid grounds for remarriage after divorce—entered the tradition through its father, John Calvin. In his commentary on Matthew 19:9, Calvin explained that "it is not in the power of a man to dissolve the engagement of marriage, which the Lord wishes to remain, inviolate" except that a husband or a wife who commits adultery can and does dissolve the marriage. This sets the innocent wife or husband at liberty; he or she is now free to remarry. Calvin criticized as "very ill explained" the interpretation of the second part of the text ["and whoso marrieth her which is put away doth commit adultery"] that holds that

> celibacy is enjoined in all cases when a divorce has taken place; and, therefore, if a husband should put away an adulteress, both would be laid under the necessity of remaining unmarried. As if this liberty of divorce meant only not to lie with his wife; and as if Christ did not evidently grant permission in this case to do what the Jews were wont indiscriminately to do at their pleasure.[19]

---

19 John Calvin, *Commentary on a Harmony of the Evangelists, Matthew, Mark, and Luke,* trans. William Pringle (Grand Rapids, MI: Wm. B. Eerdmans Publishing Co., 1949), 2:382–85.

An unbeliever's desertion of a believing wife or husband, as described in 1 Corinthians 7:15, Calvin saw as the unbeliever's divorcing "God rather than...his or her partner. There is, therefore, in this case a special reason, inasmuch as the first and chief bond is not merely loosed, but even utterly broken through."[20] Not only adultery, therefore, but also desertion broke the marriage bond, in the judgment of Calvin, freeing the deserted Christian to remarry.

In keeping with Calvin's thinking on marriage, divorce, and remarriage, the marriage ordinances of Geneva, drafted under Calvin's inspiration, approved remarriage after divorce on the ground of adultery, as well as the remarriage of some who had been deserted by their husbands or wives. The ordinance governing remarriage on the ground of adultery read as follows:

> If a husband accuses his wife of adultery and he proves it by sufficient witnesses or evidences and demands to be separated by divorce, it shall be granted, and thereafter he shall be able to marry again if he so wishes.[21]

Several ordinances dealt with desertion in various forms. One stated:

> If a husband who is debauched has deserted his wife without his wife having given him any occasion for doing so or being in any way to blame for it...The wife...if she is unable

---

20 John Calvin, *Commentary on the Epistles of Paul the Apostle to the Corinthians,* trans. John Pringle (Grand Rapids, MI: Wm. B. Eerdmans Publishing Co., 1948), 1:244.

21 Philip Edgcumbe Hughes, ed. and trans., *The Register of the Company of Pastors of Geneva in the Time of Calvin* (Grand Rapids, MI: Wm. B. Eerdmans Publishing Co., 1966), 77. In an even-handed way, the ordinances went on to apply this law of the dissolution of marriage by adultery to the wife whose husband has been guilty of adultery.

to discover where he is, shall wait until the completion of one year...and when the year is up she shall be able to come before the Consistory. If it is then ascertained that she needs to be married, she shall be exhorted and sent to the Council...After this the public announcements previously mentioned shall be proceeded with so that liberty may be given to the woman to remarry.[22]

It is worthy of note that the rules of Geneva governing remarriage on the ground of desertion tied desertion to "debauchery." In his magisterial study of divorce, Roderick Phillips makes a convincing case for the contention that, although Calvin recognized desertion as a second ground for divorce and remarriage, desertion for Calvin necessarily involved adultery on the part of the deserter. Essentially, then, Calvin acknowledged only one ground for remarriage: adultery.[23]

In his view that adultery and desertion were grounds for divorce and remarriage, Calvin agreed with Martin Luther. Already in "The Babylonian Captivity of the Church" in 1520, Luther proposed, although somewhat tentatively, that remarriage be permitted on two grounds.

> Christ, then, permits divorce, but only on the ground of unchastity. The pope must, therefore, be in error whenever he grants a divorce for any other cause...Yet it is still a greater wonder to me why they compel a man to remain unmarried after being separated from his wife by divorce, and why they will not permit him to remarry. For if Christ

---

22 Ibid., 79.

23 Roderick Phillips, *Putting Asunder: A History of Divorce in Western Society* (Cambridge: Cambridge University Press, 1988), 54–55.

permits divorce on the ground of unchastity and compels no one to remain unmarried, and if Paul would rather have us marry than burn (1 Cor. 7:9), then he certainly seems to permit a man to marry another woman in the place of the one who has been put away...

I, indeed, who alone against all cannot establish any rule in this matter would yet greatly desire at least the passage in 1 Cor. 7 (:15) to be applied here...Here the Apostle gives permission to put away the unbeliever who departs and to set the believing spouse free to marry again.[24]

In his commentary of 1523 on 1 Corinthians 7:15, Luther wrote:

Here the apostle releases the Christian spouse, once the non-Christian partner has separated himself or will not permit his mate to lead a Christian life, giving the former the right and authority to marry another partner.[25]

In a sermon in 1531 on Matthew 5:31–32, Luther approved the remarriage of the person divorced on the ground of the marriage companion's adultery:

But you ask: "Then is there no legitimate cause for the divorce and remarriage of a man and his wife?" Answer: Both here and in Matthew 19:9 Christ sets down only one, called adultery.[26]

---

24 Martin Luther, "On the Babylonian Captivity of the Church," in *Three Treatises* (Philadelphia: Muhlenberg Press, 1960), 236–37. Luther was here opening up a radical break with the church's doctrine and practice of marriage.

25 Martin Luther, *Luther's Works*, ed. Hilton C. Oswald (Saint Louis: Concordia Publishing House, 1973), 28:36.

26 Martin Luther, *Luther's Works*, ed. Jaroslav Pelikan (Saint Louis: Concordia Publishing House, 1956), 21:96.

The reason Luther gave for this right to remarry is significant since it shows that the reformer was convinced that in reality only death dissolves the marriage bond:

He [Christ] cites it [adultery as the only legitimate cause for divorce and remarriage] on the basis of the Law of Moses, which punishes adultery with death (Lev. 20:10). Since it is only death that can dissolve a marriage and set you free, an adulterer has already been divorced, not by men but by God Himself, and separated not only from his wife but from this very life. By his adultery he has divorced himself from his wife and has dissolved his marriage. He had no right to do either of these, and so He has brought on his own death, in the sense that before God he is already dead even though the judge may not have him executed.[27]

It is plain that beginning with the great reformers the Reformed tradition adopted and defended the view that remarriage after divorce is lawful for Christians on the grounds of adultery and desertion. Thus the tradition denied that marriage is an unbreakable bond for life established by God. The stand of the Reformed tradition implies that marriage is merely a human contract. A marriage may have been made by God, but it can be broken by the sinful deeds of men and women.

Roderick Phillips is correct when he describes the position that adultery and desertion are grounds for divorce and remarriage as "a Protestant orthodoxy" and when he asserts that the reformers "rejected the doctrine of marital indissolubility."[28]

---

27 Ibid.
28 Phillips, *Putting Asunder*, 40, 83.

Testing the Tradition

It would be a mistake, however, to conclude that the Reformed tradition on marriage, divorce, and remarriage is radically and unalterably opposed to the doctrine of an unbreakable marriage bond. The Reformed tradition is more open to such a doctrine than might be supposed on the basis of the sketch of the tradition that has been given above.

For, first, in permitting remarriage and thus repudiating marriage as a lifelong bond, the reformers were reacting against the Roman Catholic doctrine that marriage is a sacrament. Rejection of the doctrine that marriage is a sacrament was right. "Mystery" in Ephesians 5:32 is not "sacrament." Marriage is not, like the Lord's supper, a means of grace. It is a creation ordinance, not a church ordinance.

But the reformers' reaction was wrong. Denial that marriage is a sacrament does not by any stretch of the imagination imply rejection of marriage as an unbreakable bond. The simple fact is that, beginning with the institution of marriage in Genesis 2:18–25, scripture teaches the nature of marriage to be a lifelong, unbreakable bond between one man and one woman. The question whether marriage is a lifelong bond is not answered simply by denying that marriage is a sacrament. It is answered by the biblical texts, rightly interpreted. These texts include Matthew 19:9; Mark 10:11–12; Luke 16:18; Romans 7:2–3; 1 Corinthians 7:39; and Ephesians 5:32.

The reformers' interpretation of these texts is obviously erroneous. Two prominent evangelical theologians have charged, convincingly, that the reformers adopted the exegesis of the texts on marriage and divorce of the Renaissance humanist scholar, Erasmus. By taking over Erasmus' interpretation of the texts, the reformers introduced his doctrine of marriage as a breakable contract into the churches of the Reformation.

The early Christian writers' interpretation of the divorce texts remained the standard view of the church in the West until the sixteenth century when Erasmus suggested a different view that was adopted by Protestant theologians.

The Protestant Reformers latched on to Erasmus's interpretation of the divorce texts and defended his exegesis from the moment they became known.[29]

A third consideration is that the reformers definitely wanted to retain the idea of marriage as a permanent bond, inconsistent though this was with their position that the bond could be broken by adultery and desertion. In "The Babylonian Captivity of the Church," in which he permitted remarriage after divorce to the innocent party and to the deserted believer, Luther nevertheless expressed grave doubt about and strong objection to "divorce," by which he meant divorce that dissolves the marriage:

> As to divorce, it is still a question for debate whether it is allowable. For my part I so greatly detest divorce that I should prefer bigamy to it; but whether it is allowable, I do not venture to decide.[30]

Here Luther was forecasting his infamous advice to Philip of Hesse, that rather than divorce and remarry Philip secretly take a second wife, advice that scandalized Christendom. Wretched as this advice was, it did indicate Luther's aversion to divorce.

In his sermon on Matthew 5:31–32, Luther commanded Christians not to divorce and, if they did, to remain unmarried. The reason was that

---

29 William A. Heth and Gordon J. Wenham, *Jesus and Divorce: The Problem with the Evangelical Consensus* (Nashville: Thomas Nelson, 1984), 73–86.

30 Luther, "On the Babylonian Captivity of the Church," in *Three Treatises*, 235–36.

we have no right to make marriage a free thing, as though it were in our power to do with as we pleased, changing and exchanging. But the rule is the one Christ pronounces (Matt. 19:6): "What God has joined together, let not man put asunder."[31]

Calvin saw the heart of Jesus' instruction in Matthew 19:3–12 to be that "a fixed law was laid down as to the sacred and indissoluble bond of marriage."[32] In his commentary on 1 Corinthians 7:39, Calvin stated, "It is the law that declares the connection between husband and wife to be indissoluble."

This implies, said Calvin, that "a woman is bound to her husband for life," being "set at liberty by his death."[33] In a sermon on Ephesians 5:31–33, Calvin pointed out to his congregation, "We see how God even from the beginning has linked together man and wife in an inseparable bond."[34]

Phillips correctly represents the thinking of the reformers when he writes, "The Reformers rejected the doctrine of marital indissolubility far more hesitantly than they abandoned other key elements of Catholic marriage doctrine."[35]

The Reformed tradition followed the reformers in this hesitancy to let go the idea that marriage is an indissoluble bond, despite its affirmation that adultery and desertion do, in fact, dissolve the bond. Bouwman spoke of the "general rule" of the scriptures that "marriage in its essence is indissoluble."[36] Geesink

---

31 Luther, *Luther's Works*, 21:94.
32 Calvin, *Harmony of the Evangelists*, 2:378.
33 Calvin, *Commentary on...Corinthians*, 1:270.
34 John Calvin, *Sermons on the Epistle to the Ephesians*, trans. Arthur Golding (London: Banner of Truth Trust, 1973), 606.
35 Phillips, *Putting Asunder*, 85.
36 Bouwman, *"Echtscheiding,"* 11.

defined marriage as the "unbreakable bond [*onlosmakeli-jke verbintenis*] of one man and one woman."[37] The Fourth Reformed Ecumenical Synod received a report from its committee that defined marriage as "a divinely ordained relationship which God intends to be an exclusive (monogamous), permanent (life-long) and cohabitive (sexual) fellowship of love." The report continued with the assertion that "the marriage bond is in its essence unbreakable."[38] To refer to no other representatives of the Reformed tradition, John Murray began his influential work on divorce and remarriage with the forceful statement, "the marriage bond is originally and ideally indissoluble."[39]

All that was necessary was that the Reformed tradition would have taken its own understanding of the essence of marriage seriously.

There is yet another indication that the Reformed tradition is open to the doctrine of marriage as an indissoluble bond. This is the fact that the reformers and the Reformed tradition had recourse, in the face of the compelling testimony of the scriptures that only death dissolves the bond, to the absurd theory that an adulterer or a deserter should, and may, be regarded as dead.

Mighty things are accomplished by adultery! Adultery is able to put asunder what God has joined together! Adultery renders a living man or woman actually dead, not spiritually now, but physically, so that the survivor may remarry!

It may be that an adulterer ought to be put to death. But if he is not put to death, or does not die naturally, the simple, obvious, and undeniable fact is that he is not dead, but alive. And the perfectly plain testimony of holy scripture is that only death sets a

---

37 Geesink, *Van's Heeren Ordinantien*, 4:217.
38 *Acts of the Fourth Reformed Ecumenical Synod*, 69.
39 Murray, *Divorce*, 1.

married person at liberty to marry another (1 Cor. 7:39). The married person who remarries while an original marriage companion is still living commits adultery (Rom. 7:2–3; Mark 10:11–12; Luke 16:18). God joins together in the marriage bond; God severs by death the bond that he made.

The facile theory that adultery dissolves a marriage—and this was the basic notion of the reformers in their teaching of remarriage—runs seriously stuck on the gospel of grace. The married Christian whose wife or husband commits adultery, perhaps over a period of time, perhaps more than once, is permitted, if not called, to forgive the offender, to be reconciled to her or him, and to take her or him back to the marital bed and board. This is the glorious example set by the real husband, Jesus Christ, in his dealings with his wife, the church. It is fundamental to salvation that Christ does not permit the church's adultery to dissolve the real marriage, the covenant of grace.

But this makes plain that *adultery does not dissolve the bond.* If adultery dissolved the bond, there could be no possibility of the restoration of the adulterer and the continuance of the marriage. This means that, on the view of the reformers, what really dissolves the bond is the decision of the husband or wife who has been sinned against by an adulterous marriage companion. If the innocent party decides that he or she wants the marriage broken, regardless of the repentance of the guilty party, this dissolves the marriage, perhaps with the cooperation of the government. What God has joined together, the will of man can put asunder. Such a doctrine of the power of the will of man well accords with the theology of the Pelagian Erasmus, but it violently conflicts with the gospel of grace proclaimed by the Reformation.

The point here is not that every Christian whose marriage companion has committed adultery in some form or other, regardless of the conditions and consequences, is required to take the offender back and to resume living with him or her again. No one, including the church, may require this of a husband or wife whose marriage companion has committed adultery. Christ says that the person whose mate has committed adultery has the right to divorce the one who has so seriously disturbed the bond.

He or she, however, may freely forgive and gladly receive back. He or she may do so as obedience to a calling from the gracious Lord himself.

The point here is that adultery as such, on anyone's reckoning, cannot be said to dissolve a marriage. It does not have this power. The bond established by God can and does survive adultery. It has survived adultery in any number of instances in the church. Therefore, those who appeal to adultery as the ground for remarriage are required to explain exactly what it is that has dissolved the preceding marriage.

The scriptures teach that only death dissolves the marriage bond so that a married person may marry another (Rom. 7:2–3; 1 Cor. 7:39). They mean real death, the death that ends earthly life and puts the body of the dead person in the grave. If now the Reformed tradition, accepting as it does that only death dissolves marriage, would renounce the foolish notion of fictitious death, it would necessarily repudiate all remarriage after divorce, including the remarriage of the innocent party.

The reformers and the tradition that followed them must be criticized and rejected in that aspect of their doctrine of marriage that consists of the dissolving of marriage by adultery and desertion and the right of remarriage on these grounds.

The tradition, precious as it is to us, may not be allowed to override the scriptures, but the scriptures test, condemn, and purify the tradition. That the Reformed church and believer may test and reject certain aspects of their own tradition according to the standard of holy scripture is the testimony of the Reformed creed:

> We believe that these Holy Scriptures fully contain the will of God, and that whatsoever man ought to believe unto salvation, is sufficiently taught therein. For since the whole manner of worship which God requires of us is written in them at large, it is unlawful for any one, though an Apostle, to teach otherwise than we are now taught in the Holy Scriptures...Neither may we compare any writings of men, though ever so holy, with those divine Scriptures; nor ought we to compare custom, or the great multitude, or antiquity, or succession of times or persons, or councils, decrees, or statutes, with the truth of God, for the truth is above all: for all men are of themselves liars, and more vain than vanity itself. Therefore we reject with all our hearts whatsoever doth not agree with this infallible rule.[40]

The teaching that adultery and desertion dissolve the marriage bond "doth not agree with this infallible rule." The Reformed tradition has erred in its interpretation of the texts on marriage, divorce, and remarriage, especially Matthew 19:9 and 1 Corinthians 7:15.

The error has had enormous, grievous consequences. Contrary to the intention of the reformers, who restored marriage to honor and exerted themselves to strengthen the family, their view that the wicked wills and actions of men and women can dissolve marriage has seriously weakened marriage and the home throughout Protestantism.

That this would be the practical effect of their doctrine began to be evident already during the reformers' lifetimes. Appealing to 1

---

40 Belgic Confession 7, in Schaff, *Creeds of Christendom*, 3:387–88.

Corinthians 7:15, Calvin approved the divorce and remarriage of the Italian refugee Galeazzo Caracciolo, who had left his Roman Catholic wife and children behind when he fled to Geneva. The ground of the divorce and remarriage of this convert to the Reformed faith was solely the refusal of his wife to join her husband in Geneva on account of her determination to remain Roman Catholic. Leaving out of view that, in fact, the text does not authorize divorce and remarriage for anyone, by appealing to 1 Corinthians 7:15 in this case Calvin stood the text on its head: now it authorizes a believer's divorce and remarriage *on the ground of the believer's desertion of the unbeliever, indeed, of a non-Protestant.* These exegetical and marital shenanigans were the occasion of scandal. Concerning the Caracciolo case, Robert M. Kingdon notes:

> Catholic polemicists...were by this time frequently claiming that people turned Protestant and fled to places like Geneva solely to escape wives they no longer wanted and in the hope of a new sexual partner.[41]

Another ominous development already while the reformers were living was the approval, admittedly grudging, by the Protestant leaders of the remarriage of the guilty party in a divorce. Although Luther and Calvin intended to restrict the right of remarriage to the innocent party, this was found to be impossible almost at once.[42]

Reformation scholar Robert Kingdon is right when he says that "the modern explosion in divorce...[in] the twentieth

---

41 Robert M. Kingdon, *Adultery and Divorce in Calvin's Geneva* (Cambridge, MA/ London, England: Harvard University Press, 1995), 155–56. See also William Monter, *Calvin's Geneva* (New York: John Wiley & Son, Inc., 1967), 184–86, and Bouwman, "*Echtscheiding*," 8.

42 Kingdon, *Adultery and Divorce*, 89–90.

century...began in the sixteenth century...with the Protestant Reformation." The consistory of Geneva played a leading role in setting off this explosion.[43] The teaching that marriage can be dissolved by the sinful acts of men and women has led to such a disgraceful condition of divorcing and remarrying in evangelical and Reformed churches in our day as outstrips the transgressions against marriage by Rome that so offended the reformers. This doctrine of the reformers on marriage and divorce is the scandal of the Reformation. Protestants must confess it. They must then take another good, hard look at the teaching of the word of God on marriage, divorce, and remarriage.

A motivation might be that, in advocating the notion that adultery and desertion dissolve the marriage bond so that remarriage is permissible, the Reformed tradition itself broke with the Christian tradition. For some one thousand years after the apostles, the Christian church of the West, with virtually one voice, taught that marriage is an indissoluble bond.

---

43 Ibid., 180.

12

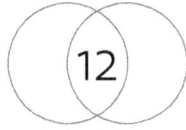

The Catholic Consensus

If, in his doctrine of marriage, Herman Hoeksema broke with the Reformed tradition, the Reformed tradition broke even more radically with the Christian tradition. For about four hundred years after the apostolic era, the catholic church taught that the marriage bond was unbreakable. There might be divorce in the sense of a full separation on the ground of the adultery of one's mate, but remarriage after divorce was forbidden. Not even the innocent party in a divorce was permitted to remarry. In the years that followed, the church of the East relaxed its doctrine of marriage to permit divorce and remarriage for many reasons. But the church of the West maintained the stand of the early church, although not without struggle.

In their doctrine of marriage, therefore, the reformers broke with the catholic consensus that had held for a thousand years or more after the apostles.[1] Thus the reformers clearly violated their

---

1 I speak of the time of the consensus as approximately a thousand years in view of the fact that in the twelfth century the doctrine of marriage as a sacrament that was later confessed by the Roman Catholic Church at the Council of Trent began to take definite shape. See Jack Dominian, *Christian Marriage* (London: Darton, Longman & Todd, 1967), 32.

own canon that the Reformation returned to the doctrines and practices of the early church, especially the doctrine of Augustine.

Herman Hoeksema's departure from the Reformed tradition, therefore, was a return, not only to the teaching of holy scripture but also to the Christian tradition of the fathers and the post-apostolic church.

The Doctrine of the Fathers

Very soon after the death of the last apostle, Hermas testified to the nature of marriage as an unbreakable bond for life. Hermas' "The Shepherd" is dated as early as AD 75 and not later than AD 165. There is reason to think that Hermas reflects the earliest church's understanding of the teaching on marriage and remarriage by Jesus and the apostles. In an imaginary conversation between an angel and himself, Hermas taught that remarriage after divorce was forbidden to a believer, even though the divorce was due to the adultery of one's marriage companion.

> "Lord," I said, "if a man has a wife who believes in the Lord and he catches her in adultery does the man sin if he continues to live with her?" "As long as the man is unaware," he said, "he does not sin. But if he discovers her sin and the woman does not repent, but rather persists in her adultery the man shares the guilt of her sin and participates in her adultery if he continues to live with her." "What, then," I said, "will the man do, Lord, if the woman persists in this passion?" "He must dismiss her," he said, "and the man must live by himself. But if, after dismissing her, he should marry another woman, he himself commits adultery."[2]

---

2 Cited in *Marriage in the Early Church*, trans. and ed. David G. Hunter (Minneapolis: Fortress, 1992), 29.

Writing at the end of the second century Clement of Alexandria explained that

> scripture recommends marriage and does not allow release from the union; this is evident from the precept: You shall not put away your wife, except because of fornication. It is regarded as adultery if either of the separated partners marries, while the other is alive.[3]

Oscar D. Watkins pointed out that in his *Stromata* Clement made clear that when he prohibited remarriage he had in view "the case of the innocent husband who has put away an adulterous wife." Watkins concluded that "in the opinion of S. Clement, the apostles understood our Lord, as he [Clement] himself understood Him, to bar all remarriage."[4]

The comment by Origen is telling. He is explaining Matthew 19. Noting that some rulers of the church have permitted a man to marry a woman whose husband was yet living, Origen adds, "thus doing contrary to the Scripture [and] to what was enacted and written from the beginning." Even though he is interpreting Matthew 19:9 with its now controversial exception clause, Origen finds no justification for the remarriage in the exception clause. Instead, he suggests that the remarriage was a concession by the rulers of the church to hardness of heart, as was the case with Moses' permission of divorce under the old covenant.[5]

---

3 Cited in ibid., 49.

4 Oscar D. Watkins, *Holy Matrimony: A Treatise on the Divine Laws of Marriage* (London: Rivington, Percival and Co., 1895), 203. See Willy Rordorf, "Marriage in the New Testament and in the Early Church," *Journal of Ecclesiastical History* 20 (1969): 204: "Remarriage during the lifetime of a previous marriage partner always remains excluded as we see from...Clement of Alexandria."

5 See Watkins, *Holy Matrimony*, 212–14. Origen is referring to Jesus' condemnation of the unbelieving Jews in Matthew 19:8. Origen wrote early in the third century.

For church father Tertullian, it was an established fact that scripture forbids remarriage after divorce, including the remarriage of the innocent party.

> But another reason…moved the will of God to prohibit divorce: the fact that (he) who shall have dismissed his wife, except on the ground of adultery makes her commit adultery; and (he) who shall have married a (woman) dismissed by her husband, of course commits adultery. A divorced woman cannot even marry legitimately; and if she commit any such act without the name of marriage, does it not fall under the category of adultery in that adultery is crime in the way of marriage? Such is God's verdict, within straiter limits than men's, that universally, whether through marriage or promiscuously, the admission of a second man (to intercourse) is pronounced adultery by Him.[6]

The reason for this verdict, said Tertullian, is the nature of marriage as an indissoluble bond by the act of God:

> For let us see what marriage is in the eye of God; and thus we shall learn what adultery equally is. Marriage is (this): when God joins "two into one flesh"; or else, finding (them already) joined in the same flesh, has given His seal to the conjunction. Adultery is (this): when, the two having been—in whatsoever way—*dis*joined, other—nay, rather alien—flesh is mingled (with either): flesh concerning which it cannot be affirmed, "This is flesh out of my flesh, and this bone out of my bones." For this, once for

---

6 Tertullian, "On Monogamy," in *The Ante-Nicene Fathers* (Edinburgh: T & T Clark, 1885; American repr., Grand Rapids, MI: Wm. B. Eerdmans Publishing Co., n.d.), 4:66.

all done and pronounced, as from the beginning, so now too, cannot apply to "other" flesh.[7]

It is true that Tertullian erroneously extended the binding of marriage beyond death so that a widow was forbidden to marry again. Nevertheless, this was an illegitimate application of Tertullian's basic understanding of scripture's doctrine of marriage as an unbreakable bond.[8]

Watkins summed up Tertullian's doctrine this way:

> He understands our Lord to permit the husband to put away for *adulterium*; he implies in addressing Marcion that the husband is bound to put away a wife living in adultery, since he would otherwise partake of her sin; he admits that the wife is at liberty to put away her husband for the same cause; he understands by *adulterium* post-nuptial adultery, "a crime incident to the marriage state"; he is positive that there is no remarriage possible for either of the separated parties, and he assumes that such impossibility of remarriage is recognised without question by all Christians alike.[9]

Augustine

Augustine wrote two treatises on marriage, "The Good of Marriage" [*De bono coniugali*] in AD 401 and "Adulterous Marriages" [*De incompetentibus nuptiis*] in AD 419. In "The Good of Marriage," Augustine set forth marriage as a lifelong, unbreakable bond:

---

7 Ibid.

8 Before writing "On Monogamy" Tertullian had recognized scripture's permitting of a widow to marry again (1 Cor. 7:39). By AD 217 Tertullian had been influenced adversely by Montanism. See Hunter, "Introduction," in *Marriage in the Early Church*, 10–11.

9 Watkins, *Holy Matrimony*, 212.

The marriage of male and female is something good. This union divine Scripture so commands that it is not permitted a woman who has been dismissed by her husband to marry again, as long as her husband lives, nor is it permitted a man who has been dismissed by his wife to marry again, unless she who left has died.[10]

Recognizing the right of the husband to divorce an adulterous wife according to Matthew 5:32, Augustine asked whether "it is accordingly permitted, after she has been put away, to marry another." Augustine denied that this is permitted:

The Apostle says [in 1 Corinthians 7:10–11] that according to the command of the Lord a wife is not to depart from her husband, but, if she departs, she ought to remain unmarried or be reconciled to her husband. She surely ought not to withdraw and remain unmarried except in the case of an adulterous husband, lest, by withdrawing from him who is not an adulterer, she causes him to commit adultery...But I do not see how a man can have freedom to marry another if he leaves an adulteress, since a woman does not have freedom to marry another if she leaves an adulterer.[11]

This statement by Augustine is extremely important not only for its express denial that the innocent party may remarry, but also for its recognition that 1 Corinthians 7:10–11 refers to a wife's

---

10 Augustine, "The Good of Marriage," trans. Charles T. Wilcox, in *The Fathers of the Church* (Washington, DC: The Catholic University of America Press, 1955; repr. 1969), 27:12.

11 Augustine, "The Good of Marriage," in ibid., 27:18.

leaving or divorcing her husband on the ground of his adultery, or "fornication," as Jesus described the sin in Matthew 5:31–32 and in Matthew 19:9. Thus, as Augustine explains, 1 Corinthians 7:15 is explicit, incontrovertible proof that the innocent party is forbidden to remarry.

Since only death dissolves the bond of marriage, all remarriage after divorce is adultery when the original marriage companion is yet living:

> Once, however, marriage is entered upon in the City [that is, church] of our God, where also from the first union of the two human beings marriage bears a kind of sacred bond, it can be dissolved in no way except by the death of one of the parties... If they do unite [with others], they commit adultery with the ones with whom they join themselves, for they remain married people.[12]

The main issue in "Adulterous Marriages" was the question whether the innocent party may remarry. Earlier, in his commentary on Matthew 19:9, Augustine had explained the exception clause, "except it be for fornication," as giving a ground only for divorce, understood in the sense of a separation of the married persons. Augustine had denied that the words "except it be for fornication" permit the innocent party to remarry.

> But in reference to what He says, "Whosoever shall marry her that is divorced committeth adultery," it may be asked whether she also who is married commits adultery in the same way as he does who marries her. For she also is commanded to remain unmarried, or be reconciled to her

---

12 Augustine, "The Good of Marriage," in ibid., 27:31.

husband; but this in the case of her departing from her husband…It is much less easy to discover how, when a man and woman have intercourse one with another with equal consent, one of them should be an adulterer, and the other not. To this is to be added the consideration, that if he commits adultery by marrying her who is divorced from her husband (although she does not put away, but is put away), she causes him to commit adultery, which nevertheless the Lord forbids. And hence we infer that, whether she has been put away or has put away her husband, it is necessary for her to remain unmarried, or be reconciled to her husband.[13]

Augustine's argument here is the one that is devastating to the interpretation of Matthew 19:9 that views the text as permitting the remarriage of the innocent party. The woman in the second part of the text is an innocent party. But Jesus forbids her to remarry: "whoso marrieth her which is put away doth commit adultery." The man who marries the innocent party commits adultery. But in the nature of the case, he cannot commit adultery by himself. At the very least, says our church father, the woman, the innocent party, causes the man who marries her to commit adultery, and this also is forbidden.[14]

Pollentius challenged this interpretation, arguing that the innocent party is permitted to remarry. "Adulterous Marriages" was Augustine's response.

In light of the teaching of the other gospels on remarriage and in light of the apostle's teaching in 1 Corinthians 7:10–11,

---

13 Augustine, "Our Lord's Sermon on the Mount," trans. William Findlay, in *A Select Library of the Nicene and Post-Nicene Fathers of the Christian Church*, ed. Philip Schaff (Grand Rapids, MI: Wm. B. Eerdmans Publishing Co.; repr., 1979), 6:20–21.

14 See Augustine's commentary on Matthew 5:31–32, in ibid., 6:17.

Augustine insisted that Matthew 19:9 may not be understood as approving the remarriage of the innocent party.

> It cannot be correctly affirmed either that the husband who puts away his wife because of immorality and marries another does not commit adultery. For there is adultery, also, on the part of those who marry others after the repudiation of their former wives because of immorality...We do not...acquit of the crime [of adultery] the one who marries a woman who has been put away on account of immorality, and we also have not the slightest doubt that each of them is an adulterer.[15]

The remarriage of the innocent party, as well as that of a guilty party, is adultery:

> We likewise declare him to be an adulterer who puts away his wife without the cause of immorality and marries another; yet we do not therein defend from the taint of this sin the man who puts away his wife because of immorality and marries another. For, while the one offense is greater than the other, we yet recognize both men to be adulterers.[16]

> Therefore, when we read in the Gospel according to Matthew: "Whoever puts away his wife except for immorality," or, to use the better reading of the Greek: "Without the cause of immorality and marries another commits adultery," we should not immediately think that that man

---

15 Augustine, "Adulterous Marriages," trans. Charles T. Huegelmeyer, in *The Fathers of the Church*, 27:71–72.
16 Augustine, "Adulterous Marriages," in ibid., 27:72.

does not commit adultery who puts away his wife because of immorality and marries another. We should suspend judgment until we consult the accounts of the other Evangelists who have written this down for us. All that pertains to this question is not expressed in the Gospel of Matthew, but the portion contained therein is expressed in such a way that from it may be inferred the whole, that both Mark and Luke have preferred to state, in explanation, as it were, so that the sense might be understood in full. Therefore, not doubting that what Matthew says is true: "Whoever puts away his wife without the cause of immorality and marries another commits adultery," as soon as we inquire if that man alone commits adultery by taking another wife who has put away his previous spouse without the cause of immorality, or whether everyone who marries another after the repudiation of the first commits adultery, so that even the one who dismisses an unfaithful spouse is included—as soon as we place these questions, shall not our answer come from Mark: Why do you ask whether this man be an adulterer, and that one not? "Whoever puts away his wife and marries another, commits adultery" [Mark 10:11]. Will not Luke also say to us: Why do you doubt that the man who puts away his wife because of immorality and marries another commits adultery? "Everyone who puts away his wife and marries another, commits adultery" [Luke 16:18]. Therefore, since it is not proper for us to maintain that the Evangelists, in writing on one topic, disagree in meaning and sense, although they may use different words, it follows that we are to understand Matthew as having desired to indicate the whole by the part, but, nevertheless, as having held the same opinion as the other Evangelists. As a result, neither the particular man who puts away his wife because of immorality and marries another commits adultery, nor does the particular man who puts away his wife without the cause of immorality commit adultery; on the contrary, everyone who puts away his wife and marries another is most certainly guilty of adultery.[17]

Oscar Watkins summarized Augustine's view of Matthew 19:9 correctly:

He [Augustine] is not blind to difficulties of interpretation; but the conclusion is invariably the same. He knows the passage S. Matthew 19:9 in the difficult form in which we have it in the received text. He rejects the marriage of the innocent husband, which some deduce from the text, on the ground of its logical incompatibility with the rest of the teaching.[18]

In an age that was as antagonistic toward the doctrine that marriage is an indissoluble bond for life as is our own, Augustine, the pastor, did not hesitate to preach this doctrine of marriage to his congregation.

You must not have wives whose former husbands are living; nor may you, women, have husbands whose former wives are living. Such marriages are adulterous, not by the law of the courts, but by the law of Heaven. Nor may a woman who by divorce has withdrawn from her husband become your wife while her husband lives. Only because of fornication

---

17 Augustine, "Adulterous Marriages," in ibid., 27:75–76.
18 Watkins, *Holy Matrimony*, 335.

may one dismiss an adulterous wife; but in her lifetime you may not marry another. Neither to you, O women, is it granted to find husbands in those men whose wives have quitted them by divorce: such are adulteries, not marriages.[19]

Summary of the Marriage Doctrine in the Early Church

With reference to the period from AD 100 to AD 314, Watkins wrote:

There is no instance during this period of any writer referring to S. Matthew 19:9, as to an authority authorizing remarriage after divorce, or as to a difficult passage requiring to be explained away.[20]

Regarding the period from AD 314 to AD 527, Watkins noted, similarly, "The verse S. Matthew 19:9 is not cited by any writer as supporting the right of remarriage after divorce for adultery."[21] There was no appeal in the early church to Matthew 19:9 in support of the remarriage of divorced persons. With the rare exception, neither was there any appeal to 1 Corinthians 7:15, the other favorite text of those who advocate remarriage. In sharp criticism of the notion that in 1 Corinthians 7:15 Paul teaches "that a Christian partner deserted by a heathen may be married to someone else," C. Caverno wrote:

That neither Paul nor anyone else ever put such construction upon his language is evidenced by the fact that there is

---

19 Augustine, "Sermon 392," in ibid., 332.
20 Augustine, "Sermon 392," in ibid., 226.
21 Augustine, "Sermon 392," in ibid., 346.

no record in history of a single case where it was attempted for 400 years after Paul was in his grave, and the Roman Empire had for a century been Christian. Then we wait 400 years more before we find the suggestion repeated. That no use was ever made of such construction of Paul in the whole era of the adjustment of Christianity with heathenism is good evidence that it was never there to begin with. So we shall pass Paul as having in no respect modified the doctrine of divorce laid down by Christ in Mt. 19.[22]

With virtually one voice the early church rejected all remarriage after divorce, including the remarriage of the innocent party. It did so because it held the marriage of Christians to be an indissoluble bond broken only by death. This doctrine of marriage, divorce, and remarriage prevailed in the church of the West during the middle ages.

Oscar D. Watkins concluded his thorough study of the history of the doctrine of the early and medieval church on marriage with this summary:

The first three centuries afford no single instance of a writer who approves remarriage after divorce in any case during the lifetime of the separated partner, while there are repeated and most decided assertions of the principle that such marriages are unlawful...In the period from Constantine to Justinian, the Churches of the West are more decided in their prohibition of remarriage than the Churches of the East. In the West the Council of Arles and the African Code, with S. Ambrose, S. Jerome, and S. Augustine, decline to

---

22 C. Caverno, "Divorce in NT," in *The International Standard Bible Encyclopaedia*, ed. James Orr (Grand Rapids, MI: Wm. B. Eerdmans Publishing Co., 1960), 2:865–66.

admit remarriage after a divorce for adultery even in the case of the unoffending husband...Speaking generally, this period from Constantine to Justinian shews the Western Churches maintaining the entire indissolubility of Christian marriage, while the Churches of the East give an uncertain sound. From the time of Justinian the Churches of the East concede, without difficulty, the right of remarriage after divorce to the innocent husband, though not to the guilty wife. Remarriage is also allowed after divorce for many other causes assigned. In the West, from the time of Justinian, the Churches of Italy appear to have maintained the indissolubility of Christian marriage, while beyond the Alps there are traces of a long and difficult struggle with the license of the secular laws and the lax customs of the peoples. From the time of Gratian, however, the indissolubility of Christian marriage was universally acknowledged in the West. As regards the Churches of the British Isles, there was, before the Norman Conquest, some diversity of view, but from the Norman Conquest onwards the indissolubility of Christian marriage has been accepted.[23]

In the course of their own, briefer examination of the doctrine of marriage in the early church, William A. Heth and Gordon J. Wenham note:

The author of the most comprehensive study ever written on this subject contends that in the first five centuries all

---

23 Watkins, *Holy Matrimony*, 435–36. The only exceptions to the prohibition against the remarriage of the innocent party in the period from AD 314 to 527 were the layman Lactantius and an unknown writer designated as Ambrosiaster. They taught that the innocent husband might remarry after divorce. Ambrosiaster expressly denied this liberty to an innocent wife. See Watkins, ibid., 296–97, 342.

Greek writers and all Latin writers except one agree that remarriage following divorce for any reason is adulterous. The marriage bond was seen to unite both parties until the death of one of them. When a marriage partner was guilty of unchastity, usually understood to mean adultery; the other was expected to separate but did not have the right to remarry. Even in the case of 1 Corinthians 7:15, the so-called Pauline privilege which later Catholics held to permit a believer deserted by an unbeliever to remarry, the early church Fathers said that the deserted Christian had *no* right to remarry.[24]

In his recent work on all aspects of marriage, divorce, and remarriage, Anglican theologian Andrew Cornes agrees with the historical analysis of Watkins, Heth, Wenham, and Crouzel:

The Fathers are almost unanimous in understanding Christ's exception in the same way. They often write about divorce and remarriage, and concentrate more on the issue of remarriage than that of divorce. When they speak of divorce, they frequently mention the Matthean exception. When, however, they speak of remarriage, they never mention any exception (Ambrosiaster is the only clear exception up to the end of the fifth century). Their normal practice is simply to prohibit remarriage absolutely (as in Mark and Luke) but significantly they often do this in a context of quoting Jesus' divorce sayings in their Matthean form or in the course of a commentary on

---

24 Heth and Wenham, *Jesus and Divorce*, 22. The author to whom they refer is H. Crouzel. His untranslated work on divorce and remarriage in the early church is *L'eglise primitive face au divorce du premier au cinquieme siecle* (Paris: Beauchesne, 1971).

Matthew's gospel. Where they do raise the specific question of whether remarriage may be legitimate in the case of divorce for adultery, they prohibit it.[25]

Church Councils

The early church expressed its doctrine of marriage, divorce, and remarriage in official decisions of her councils and synods.

The Council of Elvira (about AD 305) ruled that

a woman baptized, who has forsaken an adulterous husband also baptized, and is marrying another, must be forbidden to marry him; and if she so marry she must not receive the communion till after the husband whom she has left be dead, unless extremity of sickness compel the indulgence.[26]

The Council of Arles (AD 314) took a decision forbidding young men who had divorced their wives for adultery to marry others:

As to those who detect their wives in adultery, and the same are baptized young men, and (so) are forbidden to marry, it is decreed that so far as may be counsel be given them that, while their wives are living, although adulteresses, they do not marry others.[27]

In AD 407 the eleventh Synod of Carthage, representing the churches in Africa, resolved that

---

25 Andrew Cornes, *Divorce and Remarriage: Biblical Principles and Pastoral Practice* (Grand Rapids, MI: Wm. B. Eerdmans Publishing Co., 1993), 306–7.
26 Watkins, *Holy Matrimony*, 216–17.
27 Ibid., 294.

according to the evangelical and apostolical discipline neither a man put away by his wife, nor a woman put away by her husband, be united to any other, but that they so abide or be reconciled to one another. If, however, they contemptuously disregard this, they are to be brought to penance.[28]

Features of the Early Church's Marriage Doctrine

Certain features of the doctrine of marriage, divorce, and remarriage in the early church should be noted. One important feature is that the fathers derived their doctrine of marriage from the biblical texts, especially Christ's words in the gospels and Paul's teaching in Romans 7:2–3 and in 1 Corinthians 7. They taught that divorce is limited to the one ground of adultery and that all remarriage is forbidden during the lifetime of the original marriage companions, not because of an abstract theory of an unbreakable bond but because they understood the Bible to teach this.

Well aware of the exception clause in Matthew 19:9, the fathers rejected the interpretation that views it as permitting the remarriage of the innocent party. Rather, they held that the exception clause qualifies only the prohibition against divorce. That is, the early fathers explained Matthew 19:9 as allowing divorce on the ground of adultery, while forbidding the remarriage after divorce of both the guilty party and the innocent party. Augustine acknowledged that the text is "difficult to comprehend."[29] Nevertheless, the exception clause does not teach that the man who remarries after putting away his wife on account of her fornication is clear of the sin of adultery.[30]

28 Ibid., 336.
29 Augustine, "Adulterous Marriages," in *The Fathers of the Church*, 27:72–73.
30 Augustine, "Adulterous Marriages," in ibid., 27:72.

One reason Augustine explained Matthew 19:9 as he did was the light shed on the text by the corresponding, and clearer passages, Mark 10:2–12 and Luke 16:18: "have not the other Evangelists treated the same matter so comprehensively that [the truth of the matter] can be understood?"[31]

First Corinthians 7:10–11 also helped to convince Augustine that the exception clause in Matthew 19:9 did not allow the remarriage of the innocent party. First Corinthians 7:10–11 only repeats for the Corinthian congregation the doctrine on divorce and remarriage that the Lord Jesus taught during his earthly ministry, that is, the doctrine found in Matthew 5 and 19, Mark 10, and Luke 16. Paul points this out when he says, "And unto the married I command, yet not I, but the Lord" (1 Cor. 7:10).

The permission granted to a wife to depart from her husband, therefore, must be based on the adultery of her husband, since this is the only ground for divorce that the Lord ever mentioned. The woman in view in 1 Corinthians 7:10–11 is the innocent party. But Paul, repeating the instruction of the Lord, forbids her to remarry: "let her remain unmarried, or be reconciled to her husband." This, said Augustine correctly, is inspired commentary on the "difficult" exception clause of Matthew 19:9: the exception clause does not allow the innocent party to remarry.[32]

The Lord, the sovereign in the City of God, forbade all remarriage after divorce. Every remarriage after divorce by his judgment is an adulterous marriage.

The biblical basis for the prohibition of all remarriage after divorce while an original wife or husband is yet living accords with the nature of marriage as an unbreakable bond. This profound

---

31 Augustine, "Adulterous Marriages," in ibid., 27:73.

32 Augustine, "Adulterous Marriages," in ibid., 27:64–70; Augustine, "Our Lord's Sermon on the Mount," in *A Select Library of the Nicene and Post-Nicene Fathers of the Christian Church*, 6:20–21.

conception of marriage Augustine and the entire early church got, not from a misconception of the Vulgate's translation of Ephesians 5:32, but from the plain teaching of the Bible in Romans 7:2–3 and in 1 Corinthians 7:39. The Vulgate rendered the Greek *musteerion* ["This," namely marriage, "is a great mystery"] in Ephesians 5:32 as *sacramentum*. But Augustine did not deduce an unbreakable bond from this suggestive Latin translation of the Greek word for *mystery*. In fact, in his main works on marriage the great African says almost nothing about Ephesians 5:32. He did not find the unbreakable bond in an implication of *sacramentum* but in the express statements of Romans 7:2–3 and 1 Corinthians 7:39.

> Assuredly, "a woman is bound, as long as her husband is alive" [1 Cor. 7:39], that is, to speak more plainly, as long as he is physically alive. The husband, being subject to the same law, is likewise bound as long as his wife is physically alive. Wherefore, if he wishes to dismiss an adulteress, he is not to marry another, lest he himself commit what he reproaches in her. And so with the wife. If she puts away her adulterous husband, she is not to join herself to another husband. She is bound as long as her husband lives. She is not freed from the law of her husband, unless he be dead, so that she will not be guilty of adultery if she has been with another man.[33]

Augustine faced the objection that the innocent party may remarry inasmuch as an adulterous wife or husband is to be considered as dead: "if a man or woman commits adultery, he or she is considered dead."[34]

---

33 Augustine, "Adulterous Marriages," in *The Fathers of the Church*, 27:106; see 102–6, 118–19, 128.

34 Augustine, "Adulterous Marriages," in ibid., 27:102–6.

With characteristic wisdom Augustine analyzed this justification for remarriage as "absurd." What it means is that husbands and wives can free themselves from their marriages in order lawfully to marry another simply by committing adultery. The procedure (and argument) runs as follows. Adultery, like death, dissolves the bond. All who are not bound in marriage are free to marry. Therefore, adulterers are free to marry by virtue of their adultery.

> Therefore...do not say that an adulterous spouse, whether husband or wife, should be considered dead...The accepted teaching is: "the woman is bound as long as her husband is alive," that is to say, as long as he has not yet departed from the body. "For the married woman is bound by the Law, as long as her husband is alive," that is to say, with body intact, "If he dies," that is, if he departs from the body, "she is released from the Law which binds her to her husband. Therefore, while her husband is alive, she will be called an adulteress, if she be with another man; but if her husband dies, she is set free from the Law (of her husband) so that she is not an adulteress, if she has been with another man" [Rom, 7:2–3]...The woman begins to be the wife of no later husband, unless she has ceased to be the wife of her former one. But, she will cease to be the wife of the former one, if he should die, and not if he should commit fornication. As a consequence, a spouse is lawfully put away because of fornication, but the bond of chastity remains. For this reason, whoever marries a woman, who has been put away, even for the reason of fornication, incurs the guilt of adultery.[35]

---

35 Augustine, "Adulterous Marriages," in ibid., 27:105.

To the practical argument for remarriage—that few can live continently, as they must who are divorced because of their husband's or wife's unfaithfulness—Augustine responded:

> We ought not to pervert or alter the Gospel of Christ on their account...Take notice of how many cases will arise, when we must permit adultery to be committed, if we acknowledge the complaints of these men. What are we to do if the wife is gripped by some chronic, incurable disease which prevents her having relations with her husband? Again, suppose they are separated by captivity or some other calamity, so that the husband knows his wife is still alive, whose favors are denied him. Do you think that the mutterings of the incontinent are to be allowed and that adultery is to be countenanced?[36]

Augustine refused to destroy the law of Christ in order to make life easier for oppressed saints. Instead he offered pastoral encouragement: "The burden of self-restraint must not terrify them. It will be lighter if it is Christ's and it will be Christ's if that faith is present which obtains from the Lawgiver the grace to do what He has ordained."[37]

The early church faced and rejected all of the arguments, pleas, charges, evasions, and absurdities that are used today to fill the churches with adulterous marriages. She resolutely maintained the rigorous doctrine of marriage laid down by Jesus Christ and his apostles. She did this in a culture—the world of darkness of that day—that was as opposed to her doctrine as is the society in which we live. Divorce was available on request. Remarriage

---

36 Augustine, "Adulterous Marriages," in ibid., 27:112.
37 Augustine, "Adulterous Marriages," in ibid., 27:129.

followed as a matter of course. In the midst of such laxity, the early church bound her members to a narrow way in the matter of marriage. And she prospered and grew.

Today, in sharpest contrast, an apostate evangelical church corrupts scripture and relaxes her stand on marriage in order to accommodate the lawless culture. Spineless evangelicals plead for removing what few restraints on divorce and remarriage remain so that men and women may not be required by the church to be unhappy for the short while of earthly life and so that the church may grow.

The worldliness of modern evangelicalism in matters of marriage, in contrast to the antithetical stand of the early church, is perfectly illustrated by the evangelical Craig S. Keener in his book...*and Marries Another: Divorce and Remarriage in the Teaching of the New Testament*.[38] Keener's avowed purpose is the refutation of that interpretation of the New Testament texts that forbids remarriage to the innocent party. Along the way, he approves remarriages "even for guilty parties."[39] "We may allow some exceptions not addressed by Matthew or Paul," that is, remarriages after divorce "for reasons other than these two exceptions [adultery and abandonment]."[40]

What motivates the evangelical to throw open the doors as widely as possible to remarriage is, first, the suffering that otherwise results for some professing Christians (Keener's chapter 1) and, second, the obstacle that is otherwise placed in the way of church growth. "How long," he asks, "will conservative churches

---

38 Craig S. Keener, ...*and Marries Another: Divorce and Remarriage in the Teaching of the New Testament* (Peabody, MA: Hendrickson, 1991).

39 Ibid., 49.

40 Ibid., 105.

be able to continue evangelizing the multitudes in our society who are divorced?"[41]

Jesus' doctrine in the gospels and Paul's doctrine in 1 Corinthians 7 must be explained away. This is done by interpreting the passages "in their proper cultural context."[42] This means that Jesus' teaching on divorce must be "qualified when applied to daily living in our culture."[43] In addition interpretation of the passages is to be governed by the present cultural conditions, specifically the presence of divorce for all kinds of reasons in modern society.[44] This is interpretation that consists of making holy scripture dance to the tune of our godless, immoral society. The result is that the restriction of remarriage by Jesus and Paul on the most liberal reading of the texts must give way to wholesale acceptance of remarriage.

This is evangelicalism today! It is the church conformed to the world. It is salt that has lost its savor. How it contrasts with the early church, which boldly confronted an equally depraved culture with the precepts of the gospel

A practical motivation for the early church's prohibition of remarriage was her desire to keep the way open for repentance and reconciliation. This appeared already in Hermas in about AD 165. Having been instructed by the angel that, although a husband must dismiss an adulterous wife, he may not remarry, Hermas asks, "What if the woman put away should repent, and wish to return to her husband: shall she not be taken back by her husband?" The reply is:

---

41 Ibid., 110.
42 Ibid., viii.
43 Ibid., 21.
44 Ibid., 104–10.

Assuredly. If the husband do not take her back, he sins, and brings a great sin upon himself; for he ought to take back the sinner who has repented...In case, therefore, that the divorced wife may repent, the husband ought not to marry another, when his wife has been put away. In this matter man and woman are to be treated exactly in the same way...Therefore has the injunction been laid on you, that you should remain by yourselves, both man and woman, for in such persons repentance can take place.[45]

Augustine taught the same: forbidding remarriage enables the innocent party to take back a penitent wife or husband. "If she repents of her gross sin and returns to conjugal chastity and breaks off all adulterous unions and purposes, I cannot conceive of even the adulterer himself thinking of her as a violator of fidelity."[46]

Marriage a Sacrament?

Contemporary Protestantism ignores this clear, powerful, virtually unanimous testimony of the early church to the sanctity and permanence of marriage. It does so by dismissing it as the Roman Catholic error or regarding marriage as a sacrament. The early church's doctrine of an indissoluble bond, then, was not the *catholic* consensus, but the *Roman Catholic* consensus.

---

45 Hermas, "The Pastor of Hermas," in *The Ante-Nicene Fathers*, ed. Alexander Roberts and James Donaldson (Grand Rapids, MI: Wm. B. Eerdmans Publishing Co., repr. 1986), 2:21–22. Hermas adds that "there is but one repentance to the servants of God."

46 Augustine, "The Good of Marriage," in *The Fathers of the Church*, 27:14; see Watkins, *Holy Matrimony*, 335.

This is an unhistorical judgment in that the early church was not Roman Catholic and in that the early fathers were not already propagating Trent's dogma of the sacramental nature of marriage. In addition this judgment misconceives Augustine's reference to marriage as "*sacramentum.*"

Augustine spoke of the marriage of believers as a sacrament. According to Augustine, it is the lifelong, unbreakable bond that constitutes the sacramental nature of marriage, and it is the unbreakable bond that forbids, indeed makes impossible, such a separation of the two as would permit remarriage.

> To such a degree is that nuptial pact which has been entered upon a kind of sacrament that it is not nullified by separation...[47]
>
> Once, however, marriage is entered upon in the City [the church] of our God, where also from the first union of the two human beings marriage bears a kind of sacred bond [*quoddam sacramentum,* (a kind of sacramental quality)], it can be dissolved in no way except by the death of one of the parties.[48]
>
> The sacrament of marriage in our time has been reduced and confined to one man and one woman, so that it is not lawful to ordain a minister of the Church unless he is the husband of one wife.[49]

---

47 Augustine, "The Good of Marriage," in *The Fathers of the Church*, 27:18.
48 Augustine, "The Good of Marriage," in ibid., 27:31.
49 Augustine, "The Good of Marriage," in ibid., 27:35.

By sacrament, however, Augustine did not mean what later Roman Catholic theology intended by sacrament.[50] He did not come to the texts on marriage in the gospels and in 1 Corinthians 7 with an *a priori* theory of the sacramental nature of marriage that he had developed from a study of *sacramentum* in Ephesians 5:32. On the contrary, whatever Augustine meant by the sacramental nature of marriage he derived from Jesus' teaching on marriage in the gospels and from the apostle's doctrine of marriage in Romans 7:2–3 and 1 Corinthians 7:39.

For Augustine the sacrament of marriage was this: when two Christians married, God by a mysterious work bound them so intimately to each other that they became one flesh for life.

Simply put, marriage is a sacrament as an indissoluble bond.

That Augustine's use of sacrament for marriage differed fundamentally from the later, Roman Catholic doctrine is readily acknowledged by competent Roman Catholic scholars. Jack Dominian, who specializes in the theology of marriage, writes that Augustine "nowhere explicitly states that marriage carries with it a special gift of grace and, in view of the fullness with which he treats this subject, it does not seem rash to conclude that this momentous truth really escaped him." Dominian calls this omission on Augustine's part "particularly regretful."[51]

The translator of Augustine's "The Good of Marriage" in the series *The Fathers of the Church* quotes G. Vasquez as denying

---

50 For Rome's doctrine of the "sacrament of matrimony," see The Canons and Decrees of the Council of Trent, 24th Session, in Schaff, *Creeds of Christendom*, 2:193–98. It is basic to Rome's doctrine that marriage is a sacrament instituted by Christ, like baptism and the Lord's supper, and that marriage confers grace. It should be remembered that the popular version of the Bible in Augustine's day called marriage *sacramentum* in Ephesians 5:32. Augustine's referring to marriage as sacrament, therefore, means no more than does our referring to marriage as mystery.

51 Jack Dominian, *Christian Marriage*, 29.

that Augustine ever "called marriage a sacrament in our sense of the term." Augustine called marriage a sacrament inasmuch as it is an "indissoluble bond" that "figure[s]…the union of Jesus Christ with his Church." He did not use the term *sacramentum* for marriage "in its technical sense of 'a sacrament.'"[52]

Protestants are not able lightly to brush aside the testimony of the early church, particularly the doctrine of Augustine, by saying, "Augustine taught that marriage is a sacrament." Of course Augustine taught that marriage is a sacrament; everyone who used the Vulgate taught that marriage is a sacrament. The question is not whether Augustine taught that marriage is a sacrament. But the question is this: was the early church, including Augustine, right in understanding Matthew 5, Matthew 19, Mark 10, Luke 16, Romans 7, and 1 Corinthians 7, as well as Genesis 2:18–25, as teaching that marriage is an unbreakable bond?

The issue for the early church was not a theory of sacrament. Nor was it the prevailing culture, or the ease of the life of church members. But the issue was the doctrine of Christ in the biblical texts.

Would God that this were the issue for evangelical and Reformed churches today.

---

52 Wilcox, introduction to Augustine, "The Good of Marriage, in *The Fathers of the Church*, 27:4–5.

13

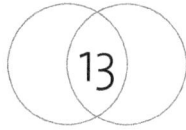

Contemporary Lawlessness

No history of the church's doctrine of marriage written today can ignore the astounding disregard for the teaching of Jesus and the apostles on marriage, divorce, and remarriage in the evangelical and Reformed churches. These churches and their theologians approve divorce for many other reasons besides fornication. They also approve, or permit, remarriage after divorce for those who divorced, or were divorced, on unbiblical grounds and even for the guilty party in a divorce, that is, the man or woman who committed adultery.

Whether these unbiblical teachings are cause or effect of the abounding, shameful practice, such is the practice of marriage in the evangelical churches in North America that the rate of divorce and remarriage is higher in these evangelical churches than in the surrounding society.

This is lawlessness not in the world, but in the churches.

Antinomianism

Appalling as this is, especially in churches that by their name evangelical or Reformed boast of fidelity to the word of God, still more appalling is the defense of this lawlessness by appeal to the gospel of grace. Theologians and churches readily acknowledge that Christ and the apostles taught marriage as a lifelong bond. They admit that divorce on other grounds than fornication and remarriage after divorce, at least for all but the innocent party, are sinful. Nevertheless, they permit these acts and receive those who are guilty of them as members in good standing in the congregations. To justify their sanction of deeds that are contrary to the law of Christ and their reception of men and women living in flagrant disobedience to the will of Christ in the most basic of all earthly relationships, they appeal to the grace of God in Jesus Christ. Grace permits one who is unbiblically divorced to live with a good conscience in an adulterous marriage, often with another man's wife.

This is not simply lawlessness. This is antinomianism. Antinomianism is the heresy that finds in grace an excuse, if not a warrant, for sinning. It is the error that denies that justification is invariably followed by sanctification. It is the false doctrine that Jehovah's prophet condemned as 'lying words" in Jeremiah 7:8–10:

8. Behold, ye trust in lying words, that cannot profit.

9. Will ye steal, murder, and commit adultery...

10. And come and stand before me in this house, which is called by my name, and say, We are delivered to do all these abominations?

It is that perversion of the gospel of grace which gleefully concludes, "[Let us] continue in sin, that grace may abound" (Rom. 6:1). Against this revolting doctrine the apostle reacted with a horrified "God forbid" (v. 2)!

The Jezebel of Thyatira was promoting fully developed anti-nomianism when she proclaimed, "Know the depths of Satan" (Rev. 2:20–24)!

Against this prevalent evangelical heresy, the truth is that the gospel of grace does not make void the law but rather establishes it as the rule of the holy life of the redeemed and thankful believer. There is, to be sure, forgiveness for those who have committed adultery, wickedly divorced, and remarried. But there is forgiveness only in the way of repentance. And true repentance never goes on happily in the sin repented of (for example, sleeping with another man's wife) but rather breaks with the sin, whatever the cost.

To assure an impenitent sinner of forgiveness, or to accept as genuine repentance a mere profession of wrongdoing that fails to show hatred and disgust for the sin by turning from it in abhorrence, is as really antinomianism as is the cry, "Let us sin that grace may abound."

In this part of our study of the history of the church's doctrine of marriage, I limit myself to the evangelical and Reformed churches and theologians. These churches and theologians claim to teach a gospel of grace that sanctifies as well as justifies. They confess Jesus as savior and Lord. They profess to honor the law of God as the authoritative guide of the Christian life. They are committed to a view of the Christian life as costly discipleship.

The Roman Catholic Church can be dismissed, regardless of its noisy, public statements on the sanctity of an unbreakable marriage bond. By its readiness to grant annulments, especially to the rich and powerful, Rome shows that it merely professes godliness in the matter of marriage while denying the power thereof. The church that grants an annulment to playboy Frank Sinatra and to adulterer Edward Kennedy and blesses the remarriages of such as these, thus accepting them as members in good standing in the

Roman Church with their new wives, is unworthy of any further consideration.[1]

The apostate, "mainline" Protestant churches pay no attention to the biblical teachings on marriage, divorce, and remarriage because they openly renounce the inspiration and authority of scripture. Marriage and sexual ethics are determined by the prevailing culture. These churches are busy drawing up and adopting reports that approve sex between consenting, unmarried adults, including homosexual sex. What interest do such churches have in what the Bible might or might not teach about divorce and remarriage?

That the liberal Presbyterian Church (USA) came to its present lawlessness in sexual and marital matters by way of antinomianism with regard to remarriage is evident from the book by James G. Emerson, Jr., *Divorce, the Church, and Remarriage*.[2] The Princeton Seminary graduate and Presbyterian minister pleaded for his church's acceptance of any and every remarried person on the ground that "realized forgiveness [dispenses with] concern for the law."[3] Again and again, he called on the church to forgive without so much as mentioning the necessity of the sinner's repentance. The brazen antinomianism that would eventually

---

1 "When Is a Marriage Not Really a Marriage," *Newsweek* (March 13, 1995): 58–59. In 1981 a Vatican commission approved a new code that "substantially extends worldwide the grounds for marriage annulment." The key article in the code adopts the criterion of "severe psychological immaturity" for annulment (*Chicago Tribune* [October 29, 1981]: 8). The shrewd church, having taken marriage into its own hands, can do anything it chooses with any marriage by means of "severe psychological immaturity." It was this kind of unscrupulous manipulation of marriage by Rome that was the reason, in part, for the reformers' rejection of what they considered Rome's doctrine of marriage, including, alas, the teaching of the unbreakable, lifelong bond.

2 James G. Emerson, Jr., *Divorce, the Church, and Remarriage* (Philadelphia: Westminster Press, 1961).

3 Ibid., 51.

lead to church approval of the vilest of sexual perversities found expression in Emerson's assertion that a remarriage after divorce is a better picture of Christ's union with the church as taught in Ephesians 5 than was the original marriage.[4]

Evangelical and Reformed churches, however, do confess to believe and teach an inspired scripture that is authoritative for the churches' doctrine and discipline and for the lives of the members. Yet these churches are increasingly lawless in the fundamental area of the Christian life that consists of marriage. They manifest themselves as antinomian, not, of course, by speaking God's word of pardon to those who truly repent of their unbiblical divorce or of their remarriage but by excusing and approving impenitent behavior on the grounds that these are not unforgivable sins and that God is gracious.

Unheeded Warnings

The gross contemporary lawlessness of divorce and remarriage has not gone unrecognized. How would this be possible in view of its public nature and in view of its calamitous consequences for the family and, therefore, for both church and society? Although he was decrying conditions in society at large, secular author Allan Bloom's searing indictment of divorcing America applies with special force to evangelical and Reformed churches.

> Of course, many families are unhappy. But that is irrelevant. The important lesson that the family taught was the only unbreakable bond, for better or for worse, between human beings. The decomposition of this bond is surely America's most urgent social problem. But nobody even tries to do anything about it. The tide seems to be

4 Ibid., 166.

irresistible. Among the many items on the agenda of those promoting America's moral regeneration, I never find marriage and divorce.

In a wicked, deadly thrust at those who divorce despite the misery that this causes their children, Bloom notes that "the divorcés are eager to get back to persecuting the wretches who smoke or to ending the arms race or to saving 'civilization as we know it.'"[5]

The same sublime hypocrisy characterizes Reformed preachers and editors of religious periodicals today. Tongue-tied with regard to the raging epidemic of divorce and remarriage that is destroying multitudes of baptized children, these champions of the social implications of Reformed religion are loud against the pernicious evil of smoking and in favor of politically correct environmentalism.

A few evangelicals have dared to speak out. Shortly before his death, Francis A. Schaeffer charged:

> Much of the evangelical church, which claims to believe that the Bible is without error, has bent Scripture at the point of divorce to conform to the culture rather than the Scripture judging the present viewpoints of the fallen culture. Do we not have to agree that in the area of divorce and remarriage there has been a lack of biblical teaching and discipline even among evangelicals? When I, contrary to Scripture, claim the right to attack the family—not the family in general, but to attack and break up my own family—is it not the same as a mother claiming the right to kill her own baby for her

---

5 Allan Bloom, *The Closing of the American Mind* (New York: Simon and Schuster, 1987), 119–121.

"happiness"? I find it hard to say, but here is an infiltration of the surrounding society that is as destructive to Scripture as is a theological attack upon Scripture. Both are a tragedy. Both bend the Scripture to conform to the surrounding culture.[6]

Carl F. Henry has similarly criticized his fellow evangelicals:

While evangelicals seek to penetrate the culture, the culture simultaneously makes disconcerting inroads into evangelical life. This is specially evident in the widening notion that divorce and remarriage are simply matters of free moral choice. The church's credibility is compromised by an evaporation of discipline even when congregational values are deeply breached.[7]

Both of these evangelical leaders put their finger unerringly on the explanation of the abounding sin of divorce and remarriage in evangelical churches, as well as the tolerance of the sin by the churches: conformity to the culture. The biblical name for this corruption of the churches in the last days is worldliness.

To their credit, some evangelicals have attempted to stem the tide of the shameful marital unfaithfulness in their circles by setting forth, persuasively, the biblical doctrine of the lifelong character of marriage. In a scholarly work that ought to have had the effect of a bombshell on the playground of American evangelicalism, William A. Heth and Gordon J. Wenham showed that Jesus and the apostles teach marriage as an unbreakable bond for

---

6 Francis A. Schaeffer, *The Great Evangelical Disaster* (Westchester, IL: Crossway, 1984), 63.

7 Carl F. Henry, *Confessions of a Theologian* (Waco, TX: Word, 1986), 388.

life. The New Testament allows divorce only on the ground of fornication, but forbids remarriage as long as both original marriage companions live. The New Testament forbids the remarriage even of the innocent party.[8]

Heth and Wenham pointed out that under the influence of the humanist Erasmus, the reformers departed from the virtually unanimous position of the early church and embraced the notion that adultery dissolves the marriage bond: "The Protestant Reformers latched on to Erasmus' interpretation of the divorce texts and defended his exegesis from the moment they became known."[9]

Meant to Last: A Christian View of Marriage, Divorce and Remarriage, a popular study of the biblical teaching on the subject, concludes by asserting that a "believer who suffers the misfortune of a divorce has two clear options: remain unmarried or be reconciled to one's mate. To teach anything else is inconsistent with God's standard for marriage."[10]

In 1993 Eerdmans published the magisterial work *Divorce and Remarriage: Biblical Principles and Pastoral Practice* by the Anglican Andrew Cornes. In this careful, thorough, five hundred-page examination of the biblical doctrine and practice of marriage, divorce, and remarriage, the Anglican vicar shows that scripture teaches marriage to be a bond that is dissoluble only by death.

---

8 Heth and Wenham, *Jesus and Divorce*. The decidedly unenthusiastic reception of the book by evangelicals and Reformed is evident from the reviews of it in *Christianity Today* (December 13, 1985) and in the *Calvin Theological Journal* 22, no. 1 (April 1987): 114–20. See also William Heth, "Divorce, but No Remarriage," in *Divorce and Remarriage: Four Christian Views*, ed. H. Wayne House (Downers Grove, IL: InterVarsity Press, 1990), 71–129.

9 Heth and Wenham, *Jesus and Divorce*, 79.

10 Paul E. Steele and Charles C. Ryrie, *Meant to Last: A Christian View of Marriage, Divorce and Remarriage* (Wheaton, IL: Victor Books, 1986), 115.

Scripture, therefore, judges all remarriage after divorce as adultery. Cornes calls on the church, particularly his own Church of England, to reject all exceptions to the rule against remarriage.[11] Reviews of this important, well-written book have been scarce. One wonders why, in view of its treating a vital issue and in light of its having been published by a major evangelical publisher. Its bulk (528 pages) should not frighten off the reader. No layman will have any difficulty with it.

From Reformed theologians and churches, however, virtually no voice is heard objecting to the abounding lawlessness of divorce and remarriage. No call goes out to the saints to honor God by honoring his institution of marriage. Much less is there a reexamination of the Reformed tradition's conception of marriage as a breakable contract, implicit in the permission of the remarriage of the innocent party, in light of the prevalence in Reformed churches of remarriage after divorce for many reasons.

Most of the Reformed, including Presbyterians, as well as many evangelicals, rather accommodate the ungodliness by advancing a permissive doctrine of remarriage that amounts to antinomianism. What writing is done on marriage, divorce, and remarriage consists of a vigorous *defense* of the increase of divorce and remarriage in the churches. Often this is accompanied by vehement denunciation of those few, feeble voices in the Reformed camp who plead for honoring God's ordinance of marriage as an unbreakable bond.

In what follows it will be shown that contemporary evangelical and Reformed theologians and churches have forsaken the Reformed and Protestant tradition that remarriage is permitted only to the innocent party for a doctrine of divorce and

---

11 Cornes, *Divorce and Remarriage.*

remarriage that permits remarriage to all, regardless of the nature of the divorce.

To the question of his Pharisee tempters, "Is it lawful for a man to put away his wife for every cause?" (Matt. 19:3), Jesus' answer today is, "Yes, indeed!" In addition he graciously permits the man who has divorced his wife for any reason whatsoever, if not to remarry his neighbor's wife, whom he has seduced, then to live in remarriage with her after he has married her. This is the new doctrine of Jesus in the teaching and lack of discipline of the evangelical and Reformed churches. This is also the obvious doctrine of Jesus in the incontrovertible fact of the church membership of these churches. The churches are filled with men and women who are divorced from their own mates for many reasons and married to the wives and husbands of others.

Evangelicals

Evangelical ethicist Norman L. Geisler holds that "the position that permits divorce for many reasons has a great deal of merit." The merit is that it encourages the remarriage of those who are divorced. Regardless of the reason for the divorce, those who divorce are permitted to remarry, because God forgives the sin of the divorce. Geisler thinks that it would be unwise, however, to permit evangelicals to divorce and remarry a second time.[12]

John Jefferson Davis teaches that "the guilty party in...a divorce may...legitimately remarry...if the guilty party has truly *repented* and attempted to make restitution for personal and financial obligations." The grace of forgiveness permits the remarriage of the guilty party. Davis states that professing Christians who "are divorced on unscriptural grounds [are] free to remarry

---

12 Norman L. Geisler, *Christian Ethics: Options and Issues* (Grand Rapids, MI: Baker Books, 1989), 277–92.

another" if they have repented and have sought reconciliation with the original wife or husband.[13]

Former Wheaton College professor Larry Richards boldly defends the position that grace permits men and women to divorce and remarry any number of times. For the church to judge anyone's divorce and remarriage as sinful would be legalism. "It is the sole responsibility of husband and/or wife to determine whether or not the marriage is really over and it is time to divorce." "Persons who divorce for any reason do have the right to remarry." Mr. Richards assures us that he would willingly officiate at the wedding of an imaginary "Tom" who was marrying after divorce "a fourth time."[14]

Writing for "conservative and evangelical Christians" Craig S. Keener contends specifically for the right of the remarriage of the innocent party. He argues that in 1 Corinthians 7:15 Paul added yet another ground for divorce and remarriage—desertion—to the one ground permitted by Christ. This implies that the biblical grounds for divorce and remarriage are not intended to be restrictive, but exemplary. Keener concludes that remarriage after divorce for reasons other than fornication and desertion is permissible.[15]

Even the guilty party in a divorce, that is, the husband or wife who is responsible for the divorce by his or her sexual unfaithfulness, is permitted to remarry.

---

13 John Jefferson Davis, *Evangelical Ethics: Issues Facing the Church Today* (Phillipsburg, NJ: Presbyterian and Reformed, 1985), 92–105.

14 Larry Richards, "Divorce & Remarriage under a Variety of Circumstances," in House, *Divorce and Remarriage*, 213–48. Richards' licentious doctrine of marriage renders the book's subtitle false: *Four Christian Views*. At least one of the views—Richards'—is un-Christian. The recent spate of books on the order of *Four Christian Views* promotes a wretched relativism regarding Christian doctrine. Are four different, violently conflicting doctrines all "Christian views"?

15 Keener, *...and Marries Another*, 105.

It is my belief, based on inference from New Testament texts about forgiveness, that the guilty parties or party are also allowed to remarry if they have genuinely repented and done their best to make any necessary restitution.[16]

The explanation is the grace of forgiveness. Grace so blots out the sin of an unbiblical divorce and of an adulterous remarriage as to justify, sanctify, and glorify the adulterous remarriage: "God's forgiveness also covers past divorces even for guilty parties, if they have repented and the marriage can no longer be recovered."[17]

The Reformed and Presbyterians

The opening of the door of remarriage widely to men and women who have divorced for any reason is especially remarkable in Reformed and Presbyterian circles. In these circles the tradition has been to restrict the right of remarriage to the innocent party in a divorce and to a believer whose unbelieving wife or husband has deserted him or her on account of the faith of the believer. Indeed, the distinctively Reformed tradition has rejected desertion as a biblical ground for remarriage, limiting the right of remarriage to the innocent party.

In recent years, as the lawlessness of divorce and remarriage increased in the world, prominent Reformed theologians and churches have advocated and approved the remarriage of those divorced for reasons other than the fornication of their mates or desertion. In a short time these theologians and churches have approved the remarriage of the *guilty* party.

The popular and highly regarded Jay E. Adams counsels his conservative audience that "remarriage, in general, is not only

16 Ibid., 200.
17 Ibid., 49.

allowed but in some cases encouraged and commanded. It is looked upon favorably in the NT."[18] To the question, "Who may remarry after divorce and under what conditions?" he answers, "All persons properly divorced may be remarried."[19] "Properly divorced," he informs us, means "those who are released without obligations."[20] In further identifying those who are "properly divorced," Adams declares that a professing Christian who has divorced his unbelieving wife contrary to the command of Paul in 1 Corinthians 7:12, may, nevertheless, be free to remarry. One improperly divorced by the apostle's standards is "properly divorced" by the Presbyterian's standards.

But this is nothing strange, for even the guilty party in a divorce may well be "properly divorced" so as to be free to remarry. Regardless whether he destroyed his marriage by his adultery "before or after conversion," if he repents, he may remarry: "Remarriage after divorce is allowed in the Bible and... the guilty party—after forgiveness—is free to remarry."[21]

Note well what this lawlessness means, and let none say that the possibility is remote, for the Reformed and Presbyterian churches are suffering this very thing. After thirty years of marriage, a man may fall in love with an alluring young lady, divorce his wife, abandon his children, marry the beauteous secretary, repent, be forgiven by the church, carry on with his new wife, and sit down at the Lord's table with orthodox Presbyterians.

It is very important, however, that his forgiveness by the elders be "note[d] in the elders' minutes book."[22]

---

18 Jay E. Adams, *Marriage, Divorce, and Remarriage in the Bible* (Grand Rapids, MI: Baker Books, 1980), 86.

19 Ibid.

20 Ibid., 86n4.

21 Ibid., 95.

22 Ibid., 96.

One thing that is plain from this sophistry is that Reformed, Presbyterian, and evangelical ministers and elders who desire to be free from the blood of the members of their congregations must do their own marriage counseling. The reputedly conservative marriage counselors, like the others, are ready to tell troubled husbands and wives what they eagerly desire to hear: you may divorce and remarry with God's blessing.

The fact is that the elders' minutes book that records the elders' forgiveness of the remarried guilty party, and thus the elders' approval of his adultery, will be brought up one day as a testimony against the elders.

In 1992 a committee presented a lengthy study on divorce and remarriage to the Presbyterian Church in America (PCA). The report was entitled, "*Ad Interim* Committee on Divorce and Remarriage to the Twentieth General Assembly of the Presbyterian Church in America."[23] Beginning with the assertion that scripture allows only the remarriage of the innocent party and of the deserted believer, the report continues by permitting the remarriage of one divorced on unbiblical grounds if his mate remarries and by sanctioning the remarriage of those who "have been in an unbiblical divorce and have already remarried."[24] The latter are to repent and rededicate their lives to Christ. The reason given for approving the remarriage of those divorced on unbiblical grounds is that "we must remember that adultery and divorce are not the unforgivable sin, but that they along with other ungodly sins are covered by the blood of Christ."[25]

---

23 *Minutes of the Twentieth General Assembly of the Presbyterian Church in America, June 15–18*, Roanoke, VA (Atlanta: The Committee for Christian Education and Publications, 1992), 513–636.

24 Ibid., 565.

25 Ibid.

The general assembly of the PCA decided to present to the ruling and teaching elders for their careful consideration the guidelines in chapter 3 of the report, "Pastoral Perspective on Divorce and Remarriage." The second guideline is "where divorce occurred prior to one's conversion, it is unclear whether the believer may remarry."[26] This is no guideline at all. It is either a charge that scripture is obscure or a confession of the ignorance of the church. But it will certainly serve to encourage the remarriage of those who are divorced for every reason, if only the divorce occurred "prior to one's conversion."

The fourth guideline permits remarriage "where a former spouse has remarried and the Session...is convinced that the parties seeking remarriage are born-again regardless of the reasons for the divorce or who was the offending party."[27] This allows the woman who broke up her marriage by her adultery—the guilty party—to remarry, if only her original husband has since remarried and if she can convince her Session that she is born again. She may well remarry her lover, if he too is now born again.

Everyone is free now to remarry: the innocent party; the deserted believer; those divorced unbiblically before conversion; and the guilty party.[28]

Such a liberating power is the forgiving grace of God in Jesus Christ.

The Christian Reformed Church in North America (CRC) had earlier come to this permissive position on remarriage after divorce. In 1956 the CRC decided that

---

26 Ibid., 588.

27 Ibid., 589.

28 Ibid., 588–89. The general assembly recommended these guidelines to ministers and elders in the PCA (2.4, 636).

people who are guilty of unbiblical divorce, or who are divorced as the result of their own adultery and having remarried, seek entrance or reentrance into the Church, shall be expected to show their sorrow and genuine repentance during an adequate period of probation.[29]

This decision represented a radical change in the stand of the CRC. Prior to this decision the CRC had restricted the right of remarriage to one divorced on the ground of a marriage companion's fornication, that is, to the innocent party. Those remarried after divorce on other grounds were declared to be living in sin and were refused membership in the church. By the 1956 decision the CRC permitted remarriage on the part of its members even though their divorces were unbiblical. Indeed, their divorces may have been due to their own adulteries. The remarriage of the guilty party was approved. Nor was this approval limited to those who might have divorced and remarried prior to any knowledge of the teaching of the word of God on divorce and remarriage. By its reference to those who might seek "reentrance into the Church," the decision embraced that member of the CRC who would commit adultery with the wife of a fellow member, divorce his own wife, marry the object of his lust, leave the church for a time, and then seek readmission to the church, expressing repentance.

The basis for this departure from its own tradition, and from the Reformed tradition generally, was a curious, twofold, negative declaration:

1. No substantial and conclusive Scriptural evidence has been produced to establish the thesis that parties

---

29 Cited in William P. Brink and Richard R. De Ridder, *1980 Manual of Christian Reformed Church Government* (Grand Rapids, MI: Board of Publications of the Christian Reformed Church, 1980), 268.

remarried, after being divorced on the ground of their own adultery, or divorced on non-Biblical grounds, are living in continual adultery.

2. No substantial and conclusive Scriptural evidence has been produced to warrant the demand that a person remarried after being divorced on the ground of his own adultery, or divorced on non-Biblical grounds, must, in order to prove the sincerity of his repentance, cease living in the ordinary marriage relationship with his present spouse.[30]

The "Guidelines for the Ministry of the Church" that the CRC adopted in 1980—to help the churches "in handling the important matters of marriage, divorce, and remarriage"—do not change the decision of 1956. They do prove that the CRC sinned in 1956 against better knowledge. For the guidelines expressly acknowledge that "God wills a lifelong unity of husband and wife in marriage" and that "the basic declaration of Scripture is that divorce and remarriage while one's spouse is alive constitutes adultery." The synodically adopted guidelines proceed, deliberately, to contradict the will of God and to ignore the basic declaration of scripture by approving and permitting remarriage after divorce, not only on the ground of adultery but also on many other grounds.

The explanation of this approval of what the CRC itself condemned as adultery is that grace voids the law.

First, the CRC thinks that repentance (itself a "grace") in an adulterer is perfectly compatible with his pursuing the pleasures of his sin without interruption. "I am sorry now that I stole my brother's wife and that I left my own poor wife, but I intend to

---

30 Ibid., 268–69.

enjoy my brother's wife as long as I live (or until I find someone else I prefer)."

Second, the CRC holds that the forgiveness that Christ gives through the gospel approves, blesses, and sanctifies the sin for which forgiveness has been received. The adultery of living in marriage with someone other than one's own wife, or with a woman who is the wife of another, is validated by forgiveness. Indeed, forgiveness causes the adultery of the forgiven sinner to be no longer adultery. It changes adultery into something else, something holy and good. God forgets the original, abandoned wife of the forgiven adulterer and the first husband of the woman with whom the forgiven adulterer continues to sleep.

Third, the CRC's implicit antinomianism appears when it defends its permission of remarriage as belonging to the church's "pastoral ministry," while warning that to refuse all remarriage that fails to meet definite standards would be a "strictly legal approach." Grace—a "pastoral ministry"—rules out the law. Law—the authoritative word of Christ and the apostles on divorce and remarriage—would compromise grace.[31]

Evidently the same error concerning the word of God on divorce and remarriage characterizes the Reformed churches in South Africa. *Orientation*, the international circular of the former Potchefstroom University for Christian Higher Education (now known as North-West University), devoted an issue to a study of marriage.[32]

The issue included a sound, uncompromising article by Neels Smit that not only opposed all breaking up of a marriage but also

---

31 For the CRC's "Guidelines for the Ministry of the Church in Matters of Marriage, Divorce, and Remarriage," see ibid., 269–74.

32 R. Swanepoel and B. J. Van der Walt, eds., "A Mirror on Marriage," special issue, *Orientation* 58–62 (December 1990–December 1991).

grounded this prohibition solidly upon the word of God. God made marriage, so that those who break up a marriage "negate the great God." God is witness at every marriage, so that those who break up a marriage deny God's presence at the ceremony. Although not a sacrament, marriage is a sign of Christ's covenant with his church; therefore, those who break up a marriage show contempt for Christ's relationship with the congregation. The covenant God uses the marriages of believers to bring forth and rear future generations of his children so that the one in the church who breaks up a marriage "demolish [es] the roof above his children's heads...He/she damages the line of the covenant stretching into the future."[33]

But the issue also included an article by Gert Kruger titled, "Marrying a Divorced Person." Kruger, too, knows the biblical doctrine of marriage.

There really are no grounds for divorce...Somebody who marries a divorced person therefore in reality marries the wife or the husband of somebody else, even though they are divorced. For that reason the Bible equals such a marriage with adultery.

This is the case "even where the divorced person concerned is the 'innocent' party in the divorce." For the "innocent" party "still belongs to somebody else."

Nevertheless, the church permits remarried persons who repent to live in the church with a good conscience, regardless of the grounds for the divorce or the circumstances of the remarriage. "The church is thus very firm in its point of view, but supple in its application of this viewpoint." The suppleness of application

---

33 Neels Smit, "Why May a Marriage Not Be Dissolved?" in ibid., 111–17.

is due to God's "forgiveness towards repentant sinners." Even though marrying a divorced person is "forbidden by the Bible" and even though the person married to a divorced man or woman is in every case "really married to someone else's husband (or wife)," God's mercy makes it possible that such a marriage is "very happy" and that it may "well succeed." Most importantly, mercy transforms the remarriage into a good and godly thing.[34]

Christian Reconstruction

The doctrine of Christian reconstruction on divorce and remarriage, with its corresponding practice, belongs in a category by itself. The leading spokesman is Ray Sutton in his book *Second Chance: Biblical Principles of Divorce and Remarriage*.[35] This work vies with the writing of Martin Bucer on the subject for the distinction of being the most licentious book on divorce and remarriage ever to appear in Reformed circles. It is certainly the most preposterous. Among the grounds for "biblical" divorce and remarriage are idolatry; blasphemy; false prophecy; witchcraft; divination; spiritism; Sabbath-breaking; sexual sins; murder, including physical abuse, desertion (physical and sexual), and the stubborn failure of a father to "provide economically for his family"; contumacy, which is defined as "rebellion to Biblical authority"; and malicious perjury.[36] The husband or wife who could not find a basis for divorce and remarriage in this list is lacking in imagination. A church committed to these principles

---

34 Gert Kruger, "Marrying a Divorced Person?" in ibid., 62–68.

35 Ray Sutton, *Second Chance: Biblical Principles of Divorce and Remarriage* (Fort Worth, TX: Dominion Press, 1988). The title page gives the subtitle as *Biblical Blueprints for Divorce and Remarriage*. This is what the Reformed faith in the world has come to: it is now offering "blueprints" to its adherents to enable, if not to encourage, them to divorce and remarry successfully.

36 Ibid., 57ff.

would be hard pressed to refuse divorce to any member who really wanted one.

The member who did manage to divorce on an unbiblical ground and subsequently remarried need not be alarmed, for in the name of Christ, Sutton offers the right of remarriage to the guilty party in a divorce as well. The sole exception is the man who has AIDS.

> May a guilty party remarry? Yes and no. No in the case of the man with a fatal, sexually transmitted disease...Yes, there can be remarriage on the part of the guilty party in other cases where he repents, pays restitution, and there are no lasting consequences that would be destructive to the new spouse.[37]

In multiplying biblical grounds for divorce, Sutton and the Christian reconstruction movement, which he accurately represents, hold the law of God in contempt. In Matthew 19:9 God the Son clearly and explicitly lays down the law that there is one, and one only, ground for divorce: the "fornication" of one's husband or wife. Even then, there may be no remarriage. The Son of

---

37 That this is done by a movement that boasts of its promotion of the law—theonomy!—is ironic. Fundamental to the discovery of myriad grounds for divorce for New Testament Christians out of the Old Testament is Christian reconstruction's radically mistaken conception of Old Testament scripture in relation to the New Testament. Those in the Reformed churches who are inclined to be favorable to the theonomy may well consider what this interpretation and application of Old Testament law does to the church's doctrine and practice of marriage, divorce, and remarriage. Straining at a gnat (fences around swimming pools and observing the dietary laws) theonomy swallows a camel (divorce and remarriage for every reason). For myself, I reject theonomy, among other reasons, because it is lawless in vital areas of the life of the church and of the Christian. Ray Sutton has taken his lead in the matter of divorce and remarriage from Rousas J. Rushdoony. See Rousas John Rushdoony, *The Institutes of Biblical Law* (n.p.: Presbyterian and Reformed, 1973), 401–15.

God expressly tells us that this is the law governing marriage laid down by God the Father from the beginning in the institution of marriage at creation (Matt. 19:4–6). Adding grounds for divorce and remarriage is lawlessness.

In approving the remarriage of the guilty party, Sutton is antinomian. For it is the grace of God in the cross of Christ that authorizes the remarriage: "Redemption makes this possible."[38] Sutton's gospel is not only antinomian, but also Arminian. In the risen Christ, God "offers a true second chance to all men through the second, or new, covenant in His blood." From this it follows (so, Sutton) that God now offers at least to all who are biblically divorced on one of the many grounds Sutton has listed a "second chance" at marriage.[39] This explains the title of the book.

The lack of seriousness of the Christian reconstructionist in treating the saint's obedient life in marriage comes out when he considers the divorce and remarriage of officebearers in connection with the apostle's insistence in 1 Timothy 3 that the bishop be "blameless" and that he "have a good report of them which are without." Sutton recognizes that a minister's or elder's divorce and remarriage "might affect his reputation inside and outside of the church." Sutton's counsel? Let the divorced and remarried minister or elder "take a leave of absence until things cool down."[40]

One erroneous, indeed heretical, argument by Sutton for divorce and remarriage is his assertion that Jehovah God himself divorced a wife, Israel, and married another wife, the church.[41] Not only is this corruption of the Christian life, but it is also a total

---

38 Sutton, *Second Chance*, 111.

39 Ibid., 105–9.

40 Ibid., 203.

41 Ibid., 112–13. General editor Gary North proposed this horrendous theology in his editor's introduction: "God divorced Israel...God soon remarried; He gained a new bride, the Church" (xii).

misunderstanding of the history of redemption and an attack on the faithfulness of God. God did indeed divorce Israel, but only in the sense that for a time he officially separated from her. He never dissolved the bond of the covenant that he had graciously established with her. How could he? He had established it by his unconditional promise and had sworn that it would be everlasting. According to his faithful word, he took Israel back as his wife. He "remarried" Israel, or to put it more accurately, restored her to full fellowship with himself. Indeed, he made the marriage a better, more intimate, more glorious bond than it had been before.[42]

The New Testament church is not a second wife in the place of Old Testament Israel; she *is* Israel. The church is the *reality* of Israel. The marriage covenant of God with Israel is not *replaced* by a marriage covenant with the church; it is *realized* in Christ with the church of elect, believing Jews and Gentiles.

God has only ever had one wife. Although he is the only perfectly innocent party, greatly offended by an adulterous wife, he did not, does not, and will not remarry. Let Ray Sutton and the Reformed in general draw implications from this grand truth for marriage, divorce, and remarriage.[43]

Sutton's heretical argument for remarriage brings out a truth that is fundamental in the debate over marriage, divorce, and remarriage. It may well be the most important truth of all. This is the truth that one's conception and testimony of marriage is necessarily related to one's conception and testimony of the

---

42 For God's divorce of Israel, see Jeremiah 3:8. For the fact that the divorce did not dissolve the marriage, see Jeremiah 3:14. For God's taking Israel back again as his wife in the living relationship of marriage, see Jeremiah 3 and Ezekiel 16:60–63.

43 On the unity of Israel and the church, including the oneness of the covenant in both dispensations, see Oswald T. Allis, *Prophecy and the Church* (Philadelphia: Presbyterian and Reformed, 1964). Biblical proof includes Acts 15:13–41; Galatians 4; Galatians 6:16; 1 Peter 2:9–10.

faithfulness of God in the covenant. Sutton reminds us that the doctrine of breakable marriage is based on and rooted in a "gospel" of a breakable covenant. Unfaithful husbands and wives in the church only reflect an unfaithful God. God, too, is a divorcing and remarrying God! This is the witness to God that is given by all the evangelical and Reformed churches that tolerate, approve, and bless remarriages after divorce, even though they are careful not to express this in so many words.

In contrast it is exactly the main argument and ground for the unbreakable bond of marriage that marriage is rooted in and reflects the faithfulness of God in Jesus Christ in his covenant of grace.

The controversy over marriage, divorce, and remarriage in the churches is at its heart a struggle for the gospel of the amazing, gracious faithfulness of the covenant God. To the natural mind this faithfulness to an unlovely Israel/church is absurd. To the mind of Christ, it is everything: the salvation of sinners whose only hope is that faithfulness and the glory of the triune God.

Summing Up

The doctrine and practice of divorce and remarriage in much of today's evangelicalism and in many Reformed and Presbyterian churches are lawless. The churches permit and approve the remarriages of many whom the churches admit were divorced and are remarried contrary to the commands of Christ and the apostles.

The churches take refuge in a gospel that is antinomian. Grace allows the unbiblically divorced to remarry. Grace allows those who are already remarried to continue in the adulterous marriage with a good conscience.

Leading evangelicals are already appealing to the churches' "gracious" acceptance of unbiblically divorced and remarried persons in support of their contention that these churches should also similarly accept practicing homosexuals. The Fuller Seminary theologian Paul K. Jewett raises the possibility, with reference to practicing homosexuals, that "the church might accept what it would be improper to its role actively to bless or to celebrate." In support of this "acceptance without celebration," he appeals to unbiblical divorce and remarriage: "An analogy might be to divorce."[44] Earlier, Jewett had argued that even though "the ideal of marriage which Jesus upheld did not allow for divorce," evangelicals must permit divorce and a subsequent remarriage for every imaginable reason, including that a married couple suppose that they are "incompatible," because of the grace of the gospel. To refuse this would be "a legalistic approach to the question of marriage and divorce." Permitting, indeed approving, divorce and remarriage for every reason ("the opportunity to begin life anew") "is what the gospel is all about."[45]

This "grace" is not the grace of the gospel of the scriptures.

The grace of the gospel of the scriptures will not welcome sinners who have lived in sin to the end into the kingdom of Christ in the day of judgment. Grace calls and empowers the forgiven sinner to walk in holiness of life. The divorced man may not remarry. Grace will enable him to live a single life. Grace calls those who are already remarried to stop living in that state that Jesus describes in Matthew 19:9, Mark 10:11–12, and Luke 16:18 as continual adultery. Grace will enable the repentant, pardoned adulterer and adulteress to do this.

It is the very nature of the grace of repentance itself that the sinner breaks with the sin that he sorrows over and confesses.

---

44 Paul K. Jewett, *Who We Are: Our Dignity as Human (A Neo-Evangelical Theology)* (Grand Rapids, MI: Wm. B. Eerdmans Publishing Co., 1996), 341–42.
45 Ibid., 283–89.

The penitent brings forth works worthy of repentance. Only this repentance is genuine. Only this repentance finds forgiveness with God, regardless of what the churches may say.

The contemporary lawlessness with its dishonoring of God, its misery for so many, and its ruin of multitudes of children ought to cause the Reformed to reexamine the position of the reformers and the Reformed tradition on marriage, divorce, and remarriage. Is not this chaos the fruit of the doctrine that marriage can be broken by human sin? Once the possibility of remarriage for the innocent party and for the deserted Christian has been allowed, is there any restraint against the remarriage also of others and even of the guilty party? Has not history proved that it is impossible to restrict the right of remarriage after divorce to the innocent party? And is not the reason evident to all? If adultery dissolves the bond of marriage, it dissolves the bond *for both parties, the guilty as well as the innocent.* And if the bond is dissolved for the guilty party, he has the right to marry another. He has the right from God himself to marry another. God's word gives to all those who are not married the right to marry.

One doctrine of marriage withstands all the pressures of this or any other age. This is the doctrine taught by Christ and the apostles in harmony with God's original institution of marriage. This is the doctrine born of God's own life with his people in Jesus Christ in the covenant.

Marriage is a bond established by God between one man and one woman for life, until death do them part. Humans cannot dissolve it.

Bibliography

Acts of Synod and Yearbook of the Protestant Reformed Churches in America 2000.

Acts of the Fourth Reformed Ecumenical Synod of Potchefstroom, South Africa 1958. Potchefstroom: Potchefstroom Herald, 1958.

Adams, Jay E. *Marriage, Divorce, and Remarriage in the Bible.* Grand Rapids, MI: Baker Books, 1980.

Allis, Oswald T. *Prophecy and the Church.* Philadelphia: Presbyterian and Reformed, 1964.

Augustine. "Adulterous Marriages." Translated by Charles T. Huegelmeyer. In *The Fathers of the Church.* Vol. 27. Washington, DC: The Catholic University of America Press, 1955; repr. 1969.

———. "The Good of Marriage." Translated by Charles T. Wilcox. In *The Fathers of the Church.* Vol. 27.

———. "Our Lord's Sermon on the Mount." Translated by William Findlay. In *A Select Library of the Nicene and Post-Nicene Fathers of the Christian Church,* edited by Philip Schaff. Vol. 6. Grand Rapids, MI: Wm. B. Eerdmans Publishing Co., repr. 1979.

Biddle, Perry H., Jr. *A Marriage Manual.* Grand Rapids, MI: Wm. B. Eerdmans Publishing Co., 1994.

Bloom, Allan. *The Closing of the American Mind.* New York: Simon and Schuster, 1987.

Bouwman, H. "*Echtscheiding.*" In *Christelijke Encyclopaedie voor het Nederlandsche Volk* ["Divorce," in Christian encyclopedia for the Dutch people], edited by F. W. Grosheide, J. H. Landwehr, C. Lindeboom, J. C. Rullmann. Kampen: J. H. Kok, n.d.

Brink, William P., and Richard R. De Ridder. *1980 Manual of Christian Reformed Church Government.* Grand Rapids, MI: Board of Publications of the Christian Reformed Church, 1980.

Calvin, John. *Commentary on a Harmony of the Evangelists, Matthew, Mark, and Luke.* Translated by William Pringle. Grand Rapids, MI: Wm. B. Eerdmans Publishing Co., 1949.

———. *Commentary on the Epistles of Paul the Apostle to the Corinthians.* Translated by John Pringle. Grand Rapids, MI: Wm. B. Eerdmans Publishing Co., 1948.

———. *Sermons on the Epistle to the Ephesians*. Translated by Arthur Golding. London: Banner of Truth Trust, 1973.

Caverno, C. "Divorce in NT." In *The International Standard Bible Encyclopaedia*, edited by James Orr. Grand Rapids, MI: Wm. B. Eerdmans Publishing Co., 1960.

The Confessions and the Church Order of the Protestant Reformed Churches. Grandville, MI: Protestant Reformed Churches in America, 2005.

Cornes, Andrew. *Divorce and Remarriage: Biblical Principles and Pastoral Practice*. Grand Rapids, MI: Wm. B. Eerdmans Publishing Co., 1993.

Dabney, Robert L. *Lectures in Systematic Theology*. Grand Rapids, MI: Zondervan Publishing House, repr. 1972.

Davis, John Jefferson. *Evangelical Ethics: Issues Facing the Church Today*. Phillipsburg, NJ: Presbyterian and Reformed, 1985.

Dominian, Jack. *Christian Marriage*. London: Darton, Longman & Todd, 1967.

Emerson, James G., Jr. *Divorce, the Church, and Remarriage*. Philadelphia: Westminster Press, 1961.

Engelsma, David J. *Better to Marry: Sex and Marriage in 1 Corinthians 6 and 7*. 2nd ed. Jenison, MI: Reformed Free Publishing Association, 2014.

Geesink, W. *Van's Heeren Ordinantien* [Concerning the Lord's ordinances]. Kampen: J. H. Kok, 1925.

Geisler, Norman L. *Christian Ethics: Options and Issues*. Grand Rapids, MI: Baker Books, 1989.

Grosheide, F. W. *Commentary on the First Epistle to the Corinthians*. Grand Rapids, MI: Wm. B. Eerdmans Publishing Co., 1974.

Grosheide, F. W. *Het Heilig Evangelie volgens Mattheus* [The holy gospel according to Matthew]. Amsterdam: H. A. van Bottenburp, 1922.

Henry, Carl F. *Confessions of a Theologian*. Waco, TX: Word, 1986.

Hermas. "The Pastor of Hermas." In *The Ante-Nicene Fathers*, edited by Alexander Roberts and James Donaldson. Grand Rapids, MI: Wm. B. Eerdmans Publishing Co. repr. 1986.

Heth, William. "Divorce, but No Remarriage." In *Divorce and Remarriage: Four Christian Views*, edited by H. Wayne House. Downers Grove, IL: InterVarsity Press, 1990, 71–129.

Heth, William A., and Gordon J. Wenham. *Jesus and Divorce: The Problem with the Evangelical Consensus*. Nashville: Thomas Nelson, 1984.

Hoeksema, Herman. "*Antwoord Op de Vraag van Hudsonville*" [Answer to the question of Hudsonville]. *Standard Bearer* 9, no. 18 (July 1, 1933): 424–26.

———. "*En Die Verlatene Dan?*" [And (what about) that deserted (woman) then?]. *Standard Bearer* 20, no. 3 (November 1, 1943): 50–51.

———. "*Hertrouwen van Gescheidenen*" [Remarriage of divorced (persons)]. *Standard Bearer* 19, no. 16 (May 15, 1943): 364–65.

———. "*Nog Eenmaal: DIE Verlatene?*" [Yet once again: (What about) that deserted (woman)?]. *Standard Bearer* 20, no. 5 (December 1, 1943): 96–98.

———. "*Nog Eens: En De Verlatene Dan?*" [Once more: And [what about] the deserted (woman) then?]. *Standard Bearer* 20, no. 4 (November 15, 1943): 74–75.

———. *The Triple Knowledge: An Exposition of the Heidelberg Catechism*. Grand Rapids, MI: Reformed Free Publishing Association, 1972.

———. *Unbiblical Divorce and Remarriage*. Grand Rapids, MI: Reformed Free Publishing Association, n.d.

———. *The Unbreakable Bond of Marriage*. Grand Rapids, MI: Sunday School Mission Publishing Society, n.d.; repr. 1969.

———. "*Vragen*" [Question]. *Standard Bearer* 9, no. 16 (June 1, 1933): 374–77.

Hughes, Philip Edgcumbe, ed. and trans. *The Register of the Company of Pastors of Geneva in the Time of Calvin*. Grand Rapids, MI: Wm. B. Eerdmans Publishing Co., 1966.

Hunter, David G., trans. and ed. *Marriage in the Early Church*. Minneapolis: Fortress, 1992.

Jewett, Paul K. *Who We Are: Our Dignity as Human (A Neo-Evangelical Theology)*. Grand Rapids, MI: Wm. B. Eerdmans Publishing Co., 1996.

Keener, Craig S. *...and Marries Another: Divorce and Remarriage in the Teaching of the New Testament*. Peabody, MA: Hendrickson, 1991.

Kingdon, Robert M. *Adultery and Divorce in Calvin's Geneva*. Cambridge, MA/ London, England: Harvard University Press, 1995.

Kruger, Gert. "Marrying a Divorced Person?" *Orientation* (December 1990– December 1991): 62–68.

Luther, Martin. *Luther's Works*, edited by Jaroslav Pelikan. Vol. 21. Saint Louis: Concordia Publishing House, 1956.

———. *Luther's Works*, edited by Hilton C. Oswald. Vol. 28. Saint Louis: Concordia Publishing House, 1973.

———. "On the Babylonian Captivity of the Church." In *Three Treatises*. Philadelphia: Muhlenberg Press, 1960.

Minutes of the Twentieth General Assembly of the Presbyterian Church in America, June 15–18, Roanoke, VA. Atlanta: The Committee for Christian Education and Publications, 1992.

Monter, William. *Calvin's Geneva*. New York: John Wiley & Son, Inc., 1967.

Murray, John. *Divorce*. Philadelphia: Presbyterian and Reformed, 1961.

Owen, John. "Of Marrying after Divorce in Case of Adultery." In *The Works of John Owen*, edited by William H. Goold. Vol. 16. London: Banner of Truth Trust, repr. 1968.

Phillips, Roderick. *Putting Asunder: A History of Divorce in Western Society*. Cambridge: Cambridge University Press, 1988.

The Psalter with Doctrinal Standards, Liturgy, Church Order, and Added Chorale Section. Reprinted and revised edition of the 1912 United Presbyterian *Psalter*. Grand Rapids, MI: Wm. B. Eerdmans Publishing Co., 1927; rev. ed. 1995.

"Report of the Committee on 'Marital Problems.'" In *Acts of the Reformed Ecumenical Synod Edinburgh 1953* (Edinburgh: Lindsay & Co. Ltd., 1953.

Richards, Larry. "Divorce & Remarriage under a Variety of Circumstances." In House, *Divorce and Remarriage*, 213–48.

Rordorf, Willy. "Marriage in the New Testament and in the Early Church." *Journal of Ecclesiastical History* 20 (1969): 204.

Rushdoony, Rousas John. *The Institutes of Biblical Law*. N.p.: Presbyterian and Reformed, 1973.

Schaeffer, Francis A. *The Great Evangelical Disaster*. Westchester, IL: Crossway, 1984.

Schaff, Philip, ed. *The Creeds of Christendom with a History and Critical Notes*. 6th ed. 3 vols. New York: Harper and Row, 1931; repr., Grand Rapids, MI: Baker Books, 2007.

Schaver, J. L. *The Polity of the Churches*. 4th rev. ed. Grand Rapids, MI: International Publications, 1956.

Shaw, Robert. *An Exposition of the Westminster Confession of Faith*. Inverness, Scotland: Christian Focus Publications, 1974.

Smit, Neels. "Why May a Marriage Not Be Dissolved." *Orientation* (December 1990–December 1991): 111–17.

Steele, Paul E., and Charles C. Ryrie. *Meant to Last: A Christian View of Marriage, Divorce and Remarriage*. Wheaton, IL: Victor Books, 1986.

Sutton, Ray. *Second Chance: Biblical Principles of Divorce and Remarriage*. Fort Worth, TX: Dominion Press, 1988.

Swanepoel, R. and Van der Walt, B. J., eds. 1991. "Mirror on Marriage." Special issue, *Orientation* 58–62 (December 1990–December 1991).

Tertullian. "On Monogamy." In *The Ante-Nicene Fathers*. Edinburgh: T & T Clark, 1885; American repr., Grand Rapids, MI: Wm. B. Eerdmans Publishing Co., n.d.

The Subordinate Standards and Other Authoritative Documents of the Free Church of Scotland. Edinburgh: William Blackwood & Sons Ltd., 1973.

Van Dellen, Idzerd and Monsma, Martin. *The Church Order Commentary*. Grand Rapids, MI: Zondervan Publishing House, 1941.

Watkins, Oscar D. *Holy Matrimony: A Treatise on the Divine Laws of Marriage*. London: Rivington, Percival and Co., 1895.

"When Is a Marriage Not Really a Marriage." *Newsweek* (March 13, 1995): 58–59.

Index of Scripture

Other Works by the Author

In addition to writing this third edition of *Marriage: The Mystery of Christ and the Church,* David J. Engelsma has authored, coauthored, and edited numerous other books and written countless articles for the *Standard Bearer* magazine and several pamphlets pertaining to Christian life.

RFPA publications written by David J. Engelsma

Battle for Sovereign Grace in the Covenant: The Declaration of Principles

Better to Marry: Sex and Marriage in 1 Corinthians 6 and 7

Bound to Join: Letters on Church Membership

Common Grace Revisited: A Response to Richard J. Mouw's He Shines in All That's Fair

Covenant and Election in the Reformed Tradition

The Covenant of God and the Children of Believers: Sovereign Grace in the Covenant

A Defense of the Church Institute: Response to the Critics of Bound to Join

Federal Vision: Heresy at the Root

Hyper-Calvinism and the Call of the Gospel: An Examination of the Well-Meant Offer of the Gospel

Prosperous Wicked and Plagued Saints: An Exposition of Psalm 73

Reformed Education: The Christian School as Demand of the Covenant

The Reformed Faith of John Calvin: The Institutes in Summary

Reformed Worship (coauthor with Barrett Gritters and Charles Terpstra)

Trinity and Covenant: God as Holy Family

Unfolding Covenant History: Judges and Ruth

RFPA publications edited by David J. Engelsma

All Glory to the Only Good God: Reformed Spirituality

Always Reforming: Continuation of the Sixteenth-Century Reformation

Communion with God: Reformed Spirituality

Peace for the Troubled Heart: Reformed Spirituality

Righteous by Faith Alone: A Devotional Commentary on Romans

The Sixteenth-Century Reformation of the Church